MEASUREMENT
AND
EVALUATION
STRATEGIES FOR SCHOOL
IMPROVEMENT

James F. McNamara
David A. Erlandson
Maryanne McNamara

EYE ON EDUCATION
6 DEPOT WAY WEST, SUITE 106
LARCHMONT, NY 10538
(914) 833–0551
(914) 833–0761 fax

Library of Congress Cataloging-in-Publication Data

```
McNamara, James F.
   Measurement and evaluation / by James F. McNamara, David A.
Erlandson, and Maryanne McNamara.
      p.   cm. -- (The school leadership library)
   Includes bibliographical references (p. ).
   ISBN 1-883001-78-1
   1. Educational evaluation--United States.   2. Education-
-Standards--United States.   3. Educational tests and measurements-
-United States.   I. Erlandson, David A.   II. McNamara, Maryanne,
1941-   .  III. Title.  IV. Series.
LB2822.75.M39   1999
379.1'58--dc21                                        99-22301
                                                        CIP
```

10 9 8 7 6 5 4 3 2 1

Editorial and production services provided by
Richard H. Adin Freelance Editorial Services
9 Orchard Drive, Gardiner, NY 12525 (914-883-5884)

FOREWORD

The School Leadership Library was designed to show practicing and aspiring principals what they should know and be able to do to be effective leaders of their schools. The books in this series were written to answer the question, "How can we improve our schools by improving the effectiveness of our principals?"

Success in the principalship, like in other professions, requires mastery of a knowledge and skills base. One of the goals of the National Policy Board for Educational Administration (sponsored by NAESP, NASSP, AASA, ASCD, NCPEA, UCEA, and other professional organizations) was to define and organize that knowledge and skill base. The result of our efforts was the development of a set of 21 "domains," building blocks representing the core understanding and capabilities required of successful principals.

The 21 domains of knowledge and skills are organized under four broad areas: Functional, Programmatic, Interpersonal, and Contextual. They are as follows:

FUNCTIONAL DOMAINS

Leadership
Information Collection
Problem Analysis
Judgment
Organizational Oversight
Implementation
Delegation

PROGRAMMATIC DOMAINS

Instruction and the Learning
  Environment
Curriculum Design
Student Guidance and
  Development
Staff Development
Measurement and Evaluation
Resource Allocation

INTERPERSONAL DOMAINS

Motivating Others
Interpersonal Sensitivity
Oral and Nonverbal Expression
Written Expression

CONTEXTUAL DOMAINS

Philosophical and Cultural
  Values
Legal and Regulatory
  Applications
Policy and Political Influences
Public Relations

These domains are not discrete, separate entities. Rather, they evolved only for the purpose of providing manageable descriptions of essential content and practice so as to better understand the entire complex role of the principalship. Because human behavior comes in "bunches" rather than neat packages, they are also overlapping pieces of a complex puzzle. Consider the domains as converging streams of behavior that spill over one another's banks but that all contribute to the total reservoir of knowledge and skills required of today's principals.

The School Leadership Library was established by General Editors David Erlandson and Al Wilson to provide a broad examination of the content and skills in all of the domains. The authors of each volume in this series offer concrete and realistic illustrations and examples, along with reflective exercises. You will find their work to be of exceptional merit, illustrating with insight the depth and interconnectedness of the domains. This series provides the fullest, most contemporary, and most useful information available for the preparation and professional development of principals.

> Scott Thomson
> Executive Secretary
> National Policy Board for
> Educational Administration

About the Authors

James F. McNamara is a professor at Texas A&M University. He holds graduate faculty appointments in the Department of Statistics in the College of Science and in the Departments of Educational Administration and Educational Psychology in the College of Education. While at Texas A&M, he has been a visiting scholar at the University of Michigan and an advanced study fellow at Ohio State University. Prior to joining the faculty at Texas A&M, he held academic appointments at Columbia University and the University of Oregon. He is the author of *Surveys and Experiments in Education Research*. Before pursuing a career in higher education he was a high school mathematics teacher in New Jersey and an administrator in the Bureau of Research in the Pennsylvania Department of Public Instruction.

David A. Erlandson is a professor of Educational Administration and Director of the Principals' Center at Texas A&M University. He has written or edited several books and monographs related to the professional development of principals and has contributed numerous journal articles on this topic. Prior to coming to Texas A&M University he served as a public school teacher and administrator in Illinois and as a professor in the school administration program at Queens College of the City University of New York. Dr. Erlandson is co-editor of the School Leadership Library and co-author of *Organizational Oversight: Planning and Scheduling for Effectiveness*, a volume in that series.

Maryanne McNamara is a supervisor of student teachers at Texas A&M University. While at Texas A&M she has been a program evaluator in the College of Education for the Texas School Leaders Program (funded by the Danforth Foundation) and a teacher of English as a second language in the College of Liberal Arts for international students enrolled in the English Language Institute. She has taught English and American Literature in Texas and New Jersey high schools and has served as the coordinator of alternative education programs in the College Station (Texas) Independent School District. Her research publications focus on improving teaching and learning in schools.

ACKNOWLEDGMENTS

The authors wish to especially thank the many colleagues from schools (principals, assistant principals, classroom teachers, and counselors) and universities (professors, graduate students, and preservice student teachers) whose insights and experiences added to this book.

TABLE OF CONTENTS

PREFACE

Many thoughts typically swirl around in principals' heads when they consider the topics of measurement and evaluation. Ever since they entered elementary school as students, and throughout their careers as teachers and administrators, measurement and evaluation have been a prominent part of their school environments. As students they were tested and evaluated, and as professional educators they have continued to have their performance assessed. Since becoming teachers and administrators, their roles in measurement and evaluation have been expanded. They construct tests, they conduct surveys, and they evaluate students and programs. Measurement and evaluation are an expected part of their daily school life, as ubiquitous as desks, bells, textbooks, and class schedules.

Yet, if they examine themselves closely, most principals are less than completely comfortable with their own mastery of the essentials of measurement and evaluation. These terms evoke visions of excellence, failure, tables of aggregated numbers, rank orderings, multiple-choice questions, and publication of test results. In fact, the sheer volume of activity that revolves around measurement and evaluation in the school is enough to make their heads swim and to make them wonder where they will find time to do what they need to do. Exacerbating the burden caused by this volume of activity is their uncertainty about the value and validity of measurement and evaluation processes and about their own ability to understand and use these processes for the improvement of education in their schools.

The authors of this text assume that measurement and evaluation are not merely inevitable processes in the school but are central to its efficient operation. They make a corollary assumption that the principal who would systematically enhance the impact of education in the school must be a master of these processes.

The authors recognize that what constitutes mastery in measurement and evaluation is often misunderstood by principals and others. Measurement and evaluation are not the same as statistics, nor do they require complex sophisticated skills for their mastery. They often use numbers and statistics to efficiently describe characteristics of a school and the people in it; but measurement and evaluation are much more basic than their numerical representations.

This volume systematically builds the basic knowledge and understanding that enables the principal to use measurement and evaluation in support of the school's mission. Measurement is used to determine the presence and magnitude of some variable in the operation of the school: the reading ability of a student, the prevalence of student absences in the spring semester, or the instructional effectiveness of a teacher. Evaluation is used to determine the merit and worth of the items we have measured and to use the information derived from our measurement to shape decisions. Mastery of measurement and evaluation processes in schools means knowing the nature and scope of factors that affect the operation of schools and using that information to move schools forward in their quest for educational excellence.

This volume takes the principal through a series of examples and exercises that develop this mastery. The principal is taught how to use national standards to determine and ensure the utility, feasibility, propriety, and accuracy of an evaluation; how to collect and use information that will serve the evaluation; and how to structure and schedule an evaluation. Then the principal is provided with a structure for mastering the basic concepts associated with measurement. Finally, the principal is provided with direction for integrating measurement and evaluation into the ongoing operation of the school.

Above all, the principal will find this book a very useful tool for accomplishing his or her daily tasks and for communicating those accomplishments to the school's various stakeholders. As the final chapter points out, this book is closely tied to the concepts introduced in the other volumes of the School Leadership Library. It is a valuable addition to it.

David A. Erlandson
Alfred P. Wilson

1

INTRODUCTION AND OVERVIEW

This book addresses the domain of Measurement and Evaluation, one of the twenty-one domains of knowledge and skill deemed necessary for the principalship by the National Policy Board for Educational Administration (Thomson, 1993). Its specific purpose is to help principals and others who assume leadership roles in the schools to better understand the importance of measurement and evaluation as a school improvement strategy.

This purpose is accomplished using six chapters that are organized into three parts. Throughout these chapters we illustrate our major themes with specific examples, knowing from the beginning that every school is different and that each requires different applications. Our illustrations are not intended as blueprints for what a particular school should do, but as clarification of basic measurement and evaluation principles that can be adapted to any school.

PART I: EVALUATION

Our task in the first part is to explain evaluation, and to support that explanation with research, theory, and exemplary practice ideas. Three chapters are dedicated to this task.

Chapter 2 provides an overview of what every principal should know about evaluation. It begins by defining what evaluation is and acknowledging that the purpose of evaluation is to improve the educational process. The central feature of this chapter is a specification and elaboration of *The Program Evaluation Standards* developed by the Joint Committee on Standards for Educational Evaluation (1994). These standards describe both the *ethical dimensions* of evaluation (What is the purpose of evaluation? Is the evaluation likely to achieve that purpose? How can I trust evaluation not to harm anyone?) and what might be called the *technical dimension* of evaluation (How can I trust the evaluation to be accurate in its findings? Are conclusions drawn from the findings justifiable?).

Chapter 3 uses an exercise in collecting information to illustrate the different types of data that are available to the principal, the different strategies that may be used to collect them, and the different information uses to which they may be put.

This exercise simulates a basic information approach to decision making that can serve the principal in all aspects of school activity. Specifically, the principal always will be faced with questions such as: What do I need to know about the school? Where can I obtain the necessary information to tell me what I need to know? How can this information be used to facilitate my decisions? How can my decision-making activity be used to improve future decisions?

Chapter 4 focuses on structuring and scheduling program evaluation. In this chapter we illustrate how a principal may plan for and structure program evaluation, how a principal may schedule evaluations of various elements of the school's total education program, and how these elements can be effectively related within the constraints of the school year. These illustrations are designed to demonstrate that effective administration of a comprehensive, integrated program evaluation is one of the most powerful leadership strategies that a principal can implement.

PART II: MEASUREMENT

The second part provides principals with an overview of basic measurement concepts, issues and strategies that have direct application on the job.

Chapter 5 accomplishes this by using a self-appraisal system. The system is constructed in a question and answer format. There are 30 questions that are organized into seven general sections. Each section reflects a primary area of basic measurement concerns. A complete inventory of questions is given in Appendix A.

Readers are encouraged to use this self-appraisal system as follows: First, read the question. Next, formulate a response. Finally, compare your response to the answer given in the book. Our answer for each question includes a direct reference to one or more basic references one can explore to get more detailed information. Thus, the appraisal system also provides a *self-study guide* principals can use to extend their knowledge and develop new skills.

PART III: APPLICATIONS

The third part explores ways in which principals can better relate measurement and evaluation to the real world of schools. The final two chapters are dedicated to this task.

Chapter 6 is explores ways that the measurement and evaluation expertise of professional colleagues can be used by school principals in collaborative problem solving. Such expertise resides in many school and community professionals. Among these are teachers, counselors, nurses, school psychologists, program evaluation specialists, curriculum coordinators, and social workers.

Although any of these professional colleagues could be our focus in this chapter, we chose to highlight how the professional expertise of school psychologists can be used in collaborative problem solving. Focusing on school psychologists has two primary advantages. First, it allows us to introduce a variety of school problems whose solutions typically involve the use of measurement and evaluation expertise. Second, this focus alerts school principals to the emerging interest among school psychologists in becoming more actively involved in school and classroom activities.

Chapter 7 references discussions of measurement and evaluation concerns in twelve other books already published in the *School Leadership Library.* Seven of these books addressed functional domains representing *personal skills* effective principals use on the job and five books addressed programmatic domains representing *knowledge* principals must have to develop specific decisions and effective courses of action.

The results of this content analysis and the summary of findings reported in Chapter 7 provide additional evidence to support two important ideas developed in the *School Leadership Library*. First, the findings support the idea that the twenty-one domains in the original NPBEA classification (Thomson, 1993) are not separate entities, but rather represent an efficient way to better understand the entire complex role of the school principal.

Second, examining the summary of findings for these twelve books contributes additional evidence to help readers better understand the importance of measurement and evaluation as a means to improve school leadership.

SUMMARY

All seven chapters of this book, dealing with the measurement and evaluation domain, were developed using the idea that principals exercise leadership both inside and outside the school by influencing others in the school community to join them in establishing an environment for school improvement. Using this collaborative approach, a school community becomes a dynamic learning organization dedicated to collectively searching for performance problems and committed to cooperatively implementing improvements that can be evaluated for effect.

PART I

EVALUATION

2

WHAT EVERY PRINCIPAL SHOULD KNOW ABOUT EVALUATION

In recent decades, as demands for accountability have grown, principals have become more and more familiar with evaluation. Teachers evaluate students, principals evaluate teachers, superintendents evaluate principals, and school boards evaluate superintendents. Beyond this, persons and groups outside the school district—state education agencies, the state legislature, and the local newspaper, to name a few—make their own evaluations of the educational productivity of the schools. As the emphasis on evaluation has increased, concerns about evaluation have also grown. How accurate are the findings of evaluations? How justified are the conclusions that are drawn from the findings? Once the evaluation is completed, how will the results be used? To what extent should they be used? Will the results be used for any useful purpose at all? What are the negative effects on people who are evaluated, and on other people involved in the evaluation? Is an evaluation worth the time, energy and money that are spent on it?

WHAT IS EVALUATION?

To answer these questions, we begin with an examination of what evaluation is. Michael Scriven, in his *Evaluation Thesaurus* (1991), notes that evaluation is "the process of determining the merit, worth and value of things, and evaluations are the products of that process" (p. 1). Using Scriven's definition, we can say that *merit* is the intrinsic value of the person, object, or pro-

7

cess being evaluated. A science teacher may exhibit merit as an outstanding teacher of advanced physics. By contrast, *worth* is the value of that person, object, or process to the institution or collective that its serves. The worth of our physics teacher will depend to some extent upon what classes she is assigned to teach, whether advanced physics is even taught in the school, and even the merit of her colleagues. *Value* represents both merit and worth. Clearly, when we consider the valuing of evaluation, we are concerned with both merit and worth.

THE PURPOSE OF EVALUATION

Having defined evaluation, we proceed to the question of the purpose of evaluation. Though a number of alternative answers may be given to this question, we take the position that the purpose of educational evaluation is to improve the educational process. We further suggest that this simplistic statement is not as self-evident as it may appear. Think for a moment, in terms of your own experience, of how evaluations are often not used for this purpose. Consider the process at different levels. What about elaborate end-of-course examinations that are given by some high school teachers? Do you know of any cases where the test results are *not* used, in any systematic way, either to prescribe future educational interventions for the students or to guide the course of future instruction? What about a principal's evaluations of a better than average teacher? Do you know of any cases where that evaluation was *not* used to assist the teacher in continuing professional development? Do you know of any valid evaluation of an *experimental* program that was totally ignored when it came to time to decide on the continuation or discontinuation of the program? Can you think of any other examples?

Closely related to questions regarding the purpose and intended impact of the evaluation are questions related to how likely the purpose and impact are to be achieved within the political and financial constraints that will inevitably be imposed upon it. Are the results of the evaluation likely to be worth the resources that will be expended on it? Could more productive results be obtained if we altered our evaluation procedures?

How likely is it that the results of the evaluation will be ignored? Do the politics of the situation dictate that, regardless of the evaluation results, the experiment is doomed to failure? (Or, worse yet, to success?)

Another set of concerns has to do with the negative impact that an evaluation may have on a person. It often seems to the persons being evaluated that evaluation is something that someone does to someone else, usually with the possibility of negative consequences if the evaluation is not favorable. Program evaluation, a type of evaluation that we emphasize in this chapter, attempts to take the spotlight off the individual and place it on the educational process in which individuals are engaged. Yet even program evaluation is often viewed as a means for judging the adequacy of the people who are implementing the program. As principals can testify, evaluation, in its various manifestations, has become one of the major sources of tension in today's schools. Evaluation in education has consequences for people because education is a people enterprise. It is a powerful tool for educational improvement, but, like any powerful tool (e.g., chain saw, bulldozer), it can have powerful negative consequences. The business of education is to help people, not destroy them. What can be done so that an evaluation will not destroy the people who are caught in the process?

These questions—about whether an evaluation is used to improve the educational process; whether it is structured to effectively and efficiently achieve its purpose; and whether it may negatively impact people—reflect on what may be called the *ethical* dimensions of evaluation. In addition to the ethical questions, evaluation raises other basic questions for the principal. What is the nature of a valid evaluation? This question may be divided into two related subquestions: How do I know that the information that has been collected in the evaluation genuinely reflects what it claims to reflect?, and How do I know that the conclusions reached by the evaluation are justified? These two questions about the validity of the evaluation reflect upon what may be called the *technical* dimensions of the evaluation.

These questions related to the technical dimension of evaluation may be considered in several ways. Consider first the formal assessment that a principal makes of an English class that the principal has observed, using a district- or state-mandated assessment instrument. Do the indicators used to evaluate the teacher's performance truly reflect what they claim to reflect? (For example, does the use of an outline of the day's lesson on the chalkboard really serve as a thought organizer for students?) Does the summary score assigned to the teacher's performance fully reflect the full range of the teacher's merit? Or are there important data, positive or negative, that the assessment system simply ignores? Or consider a teacher's evaluation of his students through a history test. Do the items on the test truly reflect the objectives of the course? Do students' scores on the test genuinely reflect their achievement? Similar questions may be asked about evaluations that take place at any level. Was the evaluation report that recommended implementation of a new mathematics program justified in its conclusions?

LEVELS OF EVALUATION

Evaluation in schools operates at two different levels. It functions at the individual level and it functions at a programmatic or systemic level. At the individual level we look at the performance of students and the performance of teachers, administrators, and other professionals. However, we are not merely concerned with individual performance; we are also concerned about how good an entire education program is. Although the successful performance of individuals is necessary for the success of the educational program, we cannot assume that program success is simply the sum total of individual successes. The situation is much more complex than that. Because the goodness of the educational program depends as much on the effective interaction of the parts as it does on the individual successes within it, we find it useful to approach evaluation in a programmatic way as well as in an individual way. No educational program is perfect. Program evaluation is the means by which a school systematically identifies, addresses, and diminishes its imperfections.

In individual evaluation, our concern is with the success of the individual. Every student must be considered as an individual, and it is the duty of school professionals to ensure that the educational needs of the student are diagnosed and met. Providing appropriate learning experiences to optimize educational attainment across the entire range of school subjects ought to be the ideal sought for every student. Knowing *where the student is* in terms of this attainment, *what the student needs* to move toward optimal attainment, and *how far the student progresses* in this attainment is the heart of student evaluation. We could make parallel statements regarding the evaluation of teachers, administrators, or other professionals.

In program evaluation, our concerns, while related to individual success, are of a different order. Here we are asking different questions: Is the educational program functioning in such a way as to maximize individual success? Does the system effectively diagnose individual needs? Does the school optimally use information to improve learning situations? Does the school successfully attract the best teachers? How effective is the school's staff development program? To answer these questions, we will need aggregate measures of individual student and teacher performance; but we will also need to know about the strategies and resources that have led to these results. Using this information about these programmatic concerns to improve the school program is the purpose of program evaluation.

The principal will need to move easily between these different levels of evaluation. He or she has an obligation to provide for the success of each student and for the success of every teacher and other professional in the school. But the principal also must take a systematic look at the entire school program and at the programs within it (e.g., the reading program, the foreign language program, a specially funded project). While the perspective the principal takes will be different depending upon the level of the evaluation, the primary concern will be essentially the same.

THE PROGRAM EVALUATION STANDARDS

As we have noted, principals are left with two very important types of questions about evaluation: questions about the *ethical* dimension of evaluation (What is the purpose of the evaluation? Is the evaluation likely to achieve that purpose? How can I trust the evaluation not to harm anyone?) and questions about what might be called the *technical* dimension of evaluation (How can I trust the evaluation to be accurate in its findings? Are conclusions drawn from the findings justifiable?). The remainder of this chapter describes a basic set of tools that the principal can use in answering these questions about the process of evaluation and about evaluations that take place in the school setting. This set of tools is provided in *The Program Evaluation Standards* of the Joint Committee on Standards for Educational Evaluation (1994).

Program evaluation has always been an important element in educational improvement, and various approaches to evaluation (briefly discussed in Chapter 4) have been used in schools since their earliest days. However, as the cost of education in modern American society has increased, and particularly since the federal government has become involved in education in a major way (beginning in the late 1950s) emphasis on program evaluation has increased. At the same time, concern about both the technical and ethical standards, by which program evaluations are judged, has also increased.

In response to these quality concerns, the Joint Committee on Standards for Educational Evaluation was formed in 1975 for the purpose of establishing standards for evaluation in education. This joint committee is a coalition of professional organizations that have a stake in the quality of educational evaluations. In 1981, the Joint Committee produced a set of standards called *Standards for Evaluation of Programs, Projects, and Materials* that laid the foundation for *The Program Evaluation Standards* (1994), as well as for the earlier published volume, *The Personnel Evaluation Standards* (1988). The Joint Committee's operating procedures were accredited by the American National Standards Institute (ANSI) in 1988, which means that any standards established by the committee and approved by ANSI become American National Standards (Sanders, 1994).

The Program Evaluation Standards established by the Joint Committee on Standards for Educational Evaluation provide an invaluable resource to the principal in organizing, implementing, and using the results of evaluation. We strongly recommend that every principal obtain a copy for his or her own professial library. The following introduction to these standards is devoted to helping the principal feel sufficiently comfortable with the standards so that they can be applied on the job and, through successive applications, become an increasingly valuable tool in leading the educational program of the school.

The Program Evaluation Standards are organized in terms of four basic attributes by which an evaluation may be judged: utility, feasibility, propriety, and accuracy. We define each of these attributes, and describe and exemplify the standards that support them. As we proceed through this introduction to the standards, you will notice the same themes emerging, in a somewhat different way, that we found in our brief consideration of the ethical and technical dimensions of evaluation. All of the information supplied on the standards is taken directly from *The Program Evaluation Standards, 2nd Edition* (Joint Committee on Standards for Educational Evaluation, 1994).

UTILITY STANDARDS

The utility standards are intended to ensure that an evaluation serves the information needs of intended users. They may be separately defined as follows:

U1 **Stakeholder Identification:** Persons involved in or affected by the evaluation should be identified so that their needs can be addressed.

U2 **Evaluator Credibility:** The persons conducting the evaluation should be both trustworthy and competent to perform the evaluation so that the evaluation findings achieve maximum credibility and acceptance.

U3 **Information Scope and Selection:** Information collected should be broadly selected to address pertinent questions about the program and be responsive to the needs and interests of clients and other specified stakeholders.

U4 **Values Identification:** The perspectives, procedures, and rationale used to interpret the findings should be carefully described so that the bases for value judgments are clear.

U5 Report Clarity: Evaluation reports should clearly describe the program being evaluated, including its context, and the purposes, procedures, and findings of the evaluation, so that essential information is provided and easily understood.

U6 Report Timeliness and Dissemination: Significant interim findings and evaluation reports should be disseminated to intended users so that they can be used in a timely fashion.

U7 Evaluation Impact: Evaluations should be planned, conducted, and reported in ways that encourage follow-through by stakeholders so that the likelihood that the evaluation will be used is increased.

FEASIBILITY STANDARDS

The feasibility standards are intended to ensure that an evaluation is realistic, prudent, diplomatic, and frugal.

F1 Practical Procedures: The evaluation procedures should be practical to keep disruption to a minimum while needed information is obtained.

F2 Political Viability: The evaluation should be planned and conducted with anticipation of the different positions of various interest groups so that their cooperation may be obtained, and so that possible attempts by any of these groups to curtail evaluation operations or to bias or misapply the results can be averted or counteracted.

F3 Cost Effectiveness: The evaluation should be efficient and produce information of sufficient value so that the resources expended can be justified.

PROPRIETY STANDARDS

The propriety standards are intended to ensure that an evaluation is conducted legally, ethically, and with due regard for the welfare of those involved in the evaluation, as well as those affected by its results.

P1 Service Orientation: Evaluations should be designed to assist organizations to address and effectively serve the needs of the full range of targeted participants.

P2 Formal Agreements: Obligations of the formal parties to an evaluation (what is to be done, how, by whom, when) should be agreed to in writing so that these parties are obligated to adhere to all conditions of the agreement or to formally renegotiate it.

P3 Rights of Human Subjects: Evaluations should be designed and conducted to respect and protect the rights and welfare of human subjects.

P4 Human Interactions: Evaluators should respect human dignity and worth in their interactions with other persons associated with an evaluation so that participants are not threatened or harmed.

P5 Complete and Fair Assessment: The evaluation should be complete and fair in its examination and recording of strengths and weaknesses of the program being evaluated so that strengths can be built upon and problem areas addressed.

P6 Disclosure of Findings: The formal parties to an evaluation should ensure that the full set of evaluation findings along with pertinent limitations are made accessible to the persons affected by the evaluation, and any others with expressed legal rights to receive the results.

P7 Conflict of Interest: Conflict of interest should be dealt with openly and honestly so that it does not compromise the evaluation processes and results.

P8 Fiscal Responsibility: The evaluator's allocation and expenditure of resources should reflect sound accountability procedures and otherwise be prudent and ethically responsible so that expenditures are accounted for and appropriate.

ACCURACY STANDARDS

The accuracy standards are intended to ensure that an evaluation reveals and conveys technically adequate information about the features that determine the worth or merit of the program being evaluated.

A1 **Program Documentation:** The program being evaluated should be described and documented clearly and accurately so that the program is clearly identified.

A2 **Context Analysis:** The context in which the program exists should be examined in enough detail so that its likely influences on the program can be identified.

A3 **Described Purposes and Procedures:** The purposes and procedures of the evaluation should be monitored and described in enough detail, so that they can be identified and assessed.

A4 **Defensible Information Sources:** The sources of information used in a program evaluation should be described in enough detail, so that the adequacy of the information can be assessed.

A5 **Valid Information:** The information gathering procedures should be chosen or developed and then implemented so that they will assure that the interpretation arrived at is valid for the intended use.

A6 **Reliable Information:** The information gathering procedures should be chosen or developed and then implemented so that they will assure that the information obtained is sufficiently reliable for the intended use.

A7 **Systematic Information:** The information collected, processed, and reported in an evaluation should be systematically reviewed and any errors found should be corrected.

A8 **Analysis of Quantitative Information:** Quantitative information in an evaluation should be appropriately and systematically analyzed so that evaluation questions are effectively answered.

A9 Analysis of Qualitative Information: Qualitative information in an evaluation should be appropriately and systematically analyzed so that evaluation questions are effectively answered.

A10 Justified Conclusions: The conclusions reached in an evaluation should be explicitly justified, so that stakeholders can assess them.

A11 Impartial Reporting: Reporting procedures should guard against distortion caused by personal feelings and biases of any party to the evaluation, so that evaluation reports fairly reflect the evaluation findings.

A12 Metaevaluation: The evaluation itself should be formatively and summatively evaluated against these and other pertinent standards, so that its conduct is appropriately guided and, on completion, stakeholders can closely examine its strengths and weaknesses.

We illustrate the value of the Program Evaluation Standards in a brief, hypothetical case study.

CASE STUDY: THE TANGERINE EVALUATION

THE EVALUATION

Barbara Madison, principal of Shannon Elementary School, had questions about the effectiveness of the holistic reading program, Tangerine Reading, that had been introduced into the school three years earlier by her predecessor. Although reading scores on the statewide reading competency assessment improved somewhat, Barbara was uncertain as to whether this could be attributed to the program or to other instructional strategies, such as curriculum alignment, that had been initiated. Furthermore, she wondered about some of the other promised results, such as improved student writing skills. Although comments from her teachers regarding the program were generally favorable, she felt that the program should be more formally evaluated by an outside evaluator.

She expressed her desire for an outside evaluator to the district's Assistant Superintendent for Curriculum and Instruction. He asked her whom she would recommend to do this. Barbara had no strong feelings about this; but, for want of a better alternative, she suggested the name of a professor at a nearby university from whom she had recently taken a course in reading instruction. The assistant superintendent, however, believed that hiring this professor would be too expensive and probably not very useful. Instead, he informed Barbara that, as part of the district's contract with Tangerine when they purchased the program, they could get free evaluation help from a consultant familiar with the Tangerine program by simply covering the cost of transportation, meals, lodging, and materials, for the evaluator. Tangerine would pay the consultant fee. Because the evaluation would take two full days on-site at the school, the cost would be less than $1000. Barbara agreed that this sounded like a good plan. The assistant superintendent agreed to take on the responsibility of contacting Tangerine Reading and making the necessary arrangements.

The consultant arrived at Shannon Elementary School about a month later. During her two days on campus, the consultant spent very little time talking with Barbara and did not ask to see the reading scores that reflected student progress in the years since Tangerine Reading had been introduced. On the afternoon of the first day, Barbara put the summarized and disaggregated reading scores in the office that she had provided to the consultant for her work station and asked the consultant if she needed anything else.

Most of the consultant's two days were spent observing classrooms and conferencing with individual teachers. On the afternoon of the second day she met with two separate groups of teachers, exploring possible professional development activities, sponsored by Tangerine Reading, that they might wish to follow in the future.

Approximately one month after the consultant's visit, the evaluator's report arrived. Barbara opened it eagerly. The forty-seven-page report contained descriptions of teaching techniques and strategies used in the various classrooms the consultant had observed and carefully documented how various teachers were implementing Tangerine Reading, in what ways they were failing to implement the Tangerine method fully, and what skills and knowledge they needed to acquire to successfully use Tangerine in their classrooms. Numerous recommendations were made for a variety of training opportunities (provided by Tangerine Reading for a fee) that would build the knowledge and skill that the teachers lacked. No reference at all was made to the students' test scores that Barbara had provided to the consultant or to any other measure of program impact on reading or writing skills.

At first Barbara was dismayed; then she was angry. She phoned the assistant superintendent, who told her that he had never seen much value in hiring an outside evaluator but that he had done it at Barbara's request. And the price was right. The suggestions that the teachers received for improving their teaching strategies were probably better than what they had gotten in their university classes on reading, and at least they hadn't shot a hole in the district's budget.

Barbara was less than satisfied with the assistant superintendent's response, but she decided that it was a battle she couldn't win and that her time would be better spent becoming sufficiently sophisticated in program evaluation so that she wouldn't be fooled again. About this time, she came across a copy of *The Program Evaluation Standards*.

As she became acquainted with the program evaluation standards, the rich explanatory information provided about them, and the Joint Committee on Standards for Educational Evaluation's guidelines for using the standards, an idea began to form. In the book was a case study that described how a metaevaluation could be conducted to determine how adequately an evaluation had met the standards. If she and her teachers conducted their own metaevaluation of the Tangerine evaluation, they would learn what had gone wrong and be in a strong position to prevent a repeat of that experience in the future. She proposed the idea to her teachers, who nominated a committee to work with Barbara in her metaevaluation of the Tangerine evaluation.

The Metaevaluation

Barbara and her committee of teachers decided to review the standards according to the way they were grouped. They looked first at the Utility Standards.

Utility Standards

Utility Standards are intended to ensure that the evaluation will serve the information needs of intended users (Joint Committee on Standards for Educational Evaluation, 1994, p. 23). They require evaluators to acquaint themselves with their audiences, define the audiences clearly, ascertain the audiences' information needs, plan evaluations to respond to these needs, and report the relevant information clearly, and in a timely fashion. Three Utility Standards seemed most germane to Barbara and her teachers as they considered the Tangerine evaluation at Shannon Elementary School: Stakeholder Identification, Information Scope and Selection, and Evaluation Impact.

Utility Standard 1:
Stakeholder Identification

The standard states that persons involved in or affected by the evaluation should be identified so that their needs can be addressed (Joint Committee on Standards for Educational Evaluation, 1994, p. 25). Barbara had never been clear about exactly what arrangements had been made between the assistant superintendent and Tangerine Reading. When she asked the assistant superintendent what specifically had been contracted for, he informed her that he had simply called Tangerine Reading and told them he wanted an evaluation, as stipulated in their contract. Tangerine gave him the name of a consultant that they had certified, and he contacted her. He told Barbara that the consultant promised that she would audit the implementation of the program and would provide a comprehensive review of how well the school was implementing the Tangerine program.

Clearly this standard had not been met satisfactorily. Barbara and her teachers were major stakeholders, as were the children at Shannon Elementary School. The consultant assumed that she knew what their needs were, but it was obvious that their needs had not been entirely known. Barbara's primary concern was whether Tangerine Reading, as it had been operating at Shannon Elementary School, was improving the reading and writing skills of students. What she received instead was an evaluation of how faithfully the Shannon teachers were following Tangerine procedures. Barbara and her teachers realized that it would be impossible to assess the impact of Tangerine if it were not being implemented as prescribed. On the other hand, they did not have any clear evidence that their goals would be reached even if the Tangerine procedures were followed precisely. Barbara realized now that she had been somewhat naive in readily agreeing to her assistant superintendent's recommendation to use a *free* evaluator furnished by Tangerine.

UTILITY STANDARD 3:
INFORMATION SCOPE AND SELECTION

This standard states that information collected should be broadly selected to address pertinent questions about the program, and should be responsive to the needs and interests of clients and other specified stakeholders (Joint Committee on Standards for Educational Evaluation, 1994, p. 37). The consultant knew about the procedures required by the Tangerine program. However, she failed to consider the needs and questions that Barbara and her teachers had about the effectiveness of the program. Barbara wished now that she had insisted that she and her teachers have a chance to communicate directly with the consultant prior to the evaluation.

UTILITY STANDARD 7:
EVALUATION IMPACT

This standard states that evaluations should be planned, conducted, and reported in ways that encourage follow-through by stakeholders so that the likelihood that the evaluation will be used is increased (Joint Committee on Standards for Educational Evaluation, 1994, p. 59). Barbara's intent in asking for the evaluation was to obtain direction for improving the reading and writing skills of Shannon students. While the consultant had provided a fairly clear plan for bringing the school's program into line with Tangerine philosophy, there was no convincing evidence that the inadequacies of Shannon teachers in implementing Tangerine Reading were linked to the attainment of Barbara's goal. Particularly distressing to Barbara was the fact that the consultant had apparently never looked at the reading and writing scores that had been presented to her. Barbara's purpose in seeking the evaluation had not been addressed, and she did not see much purpose in following the consultant's recommendations for further Tangerine training unless there were a clear likelihood that such training would produce the results she wanted. Consequently, there was little likelihood that the consultant's recommendations would be followed.

FEASIBILITY STANDARDS

The Feasibility Standards are intended to ensure that an evaluation is realistic, prudent, diplomatic, and frugal (Joint Committee on Standards for Educational Evaluation, 1994, p. 63). To comply with the feasibility standards, an evaluation should satisfactorily address issues of practicality, the role of various interest groups, and efficiency. Barbara and the teachers focused on two of the three Feasibility Standards: Political Viability and Cost Effectiveness.

FEASIBILITY STANDARD 2:
POLITICAL VIABILITY

To meet the Political Viability standard, an evaluator should elicit the opinions/positions of the various stakeholders in order to obtain their cooperation and curtail any attempts by these groups to bias or misapply the results (Joint Committee on Standards for Educational Evaluation, 1994, p. 71). Clearly the opinions of Barbara and her teachers, as the stakeholders responsible for implementing the results of the evaluation, were ignored by the consultant, with the result that the evaluation would have practically no impact at all. Similarly, the assistant superintendent, who by his own admission had never seen much reason for conducting the evaluation, was not likely to take an active part in seeing that the recommendations of the evaluation were implemented.

FEASIBILITY STANDARD 3:
COST EFFECTIVENESS

For this standard to be met, an "evaluation should be efficient and produce information of sufficient value so that the resources expended can be justified. An evaluation is cost effective if its benefits equal or exceed its costs" (Joint Committee on Standards for Educational Evaluation, 1994, p. 77). At first, Barbara and the teachers were not sure that this standard was relevant because the assistant superintendent had stated that it "didn't knock a hole in the budget." However, nearly $1000 had been spent to bring the consultant to Shannon, and that amount could have been used very effectively on the campus for any of a number of needs. In addition, there was some cost in terms of time and energy in preparing for the evaluator's needs and in listening to the evaluator's recommendations. But most important of all, the recommendations were, from the viewpoint of Barbara and her teachers, virtually useless. Any cost is too much if there is no benefit at all.

PROPRIETY STANDARDS

Propriety Standards guide evaluations so that they will be conducted legally, ethically, and with due regard for the welfare of those involved in the evaluation as well as those affected by its results (Joint Committee on Standards for Educational Evaluation, 1994, p. 81). In their consideration of the Tangerine evaluation, Barbara and the Shannon teachers considered four of these standards most relevant: Service Orientation, Formal Agreements, Complete and Fair Assessment, and Conflict of Interest.

PROPRIETY STANDARD 1:
SERVICE ORIENTATION

This standard states that an evaluation should be designed to assist organizations to address and effectively serve the needs of the full range of targeted participants (Joint Committee on Standards for Educational Evaluation, 1994, p. 83). Because the consultant never took time to find out the needs of Shannon Elementary School, as seen by the people who worked in it, the final report could not address or serve their needs.

PROPRIETY STANDARD 2:
FORMAL AGREEMENTS

This standard states that obligations of the formal parties to an evaluation (what is to be done, how, by whom, when) should be agreed to in writing so that these parties are obligated to adhere to all conditions of the agreement or to formally renegotiate it (Joint Committee on Standards for Educational Evaluation, 1994, p. 87). The lack of a written comprehensive agreement led to a misunderstanding of purpose between the consultant and the Shannon principal and teachers and resulted in an evaluation and a final report that did not meet the expectations of all the parties involved. As Barbara now realized, the lack of a formal agreement lay at the root of the other difficulties. A carefully crafted formal agreement could probably have prevented most of the other problems.

PROPRIETY STANDARD 5:
COMPLETE AND FAIR ASSESSMENT

The purpose of this standard is that the evaluation should be complete and fair in its examination and recording of strengths and weaknesses of the program being evaluated so that strengths can be built upon and problem areas addressed (Joint Committee on Standards for Educational Evaluation, 1984, p. 105). In one sense, it could be argued that in terms of the evaluation's objective, as seen by the consultant, she offered a fair assessment. However, even within this narrow focus, Barbara and the teachers believed that a more thorough report could have been delivered that included more explanation for her conclusions in terms of their impact on the reading and writing skills of the students.

PROPRIETY STANDARD 7:
CONFLICT OF INTEREST

This standard states that conflict of interest should be dealt with openly and honestly so that it does not compromise the evaluation processes and results (Joint Committee on Standards for Educational Evaluation, 1994, p. 115). Barbara had to admit that, because they did not check more thoroughly about the details of the evaluation in advance, both she and the assistant superintendent were probably at least as much at fault as the consultant. Certainly the consultant had never said anything to make them believe that Tangerine would not benefit from her recommendations. Nevertheless, it rankled Barbara and her teachers to realize that all the consultant's recommendations about additional training would funnel more money to Tangerine. They believed that this was a clear conflict of interest. Some of the teachers even stated that they may have felt more disposed to implement these recommendations for training if this information had been made clear before the evaluation began.

ACCURACY STANDARDS

The Accuracy Standards are applied in order to ensure that an evaluation reveals and conveys technically adequate information about the features that determine the worth or merit of the program being evaluated (Joint Committee on Standards for Educational Evaluation, 1994, p. 125). The evaluation must be comprehensive in the sense that it considers the full range of characteristics that are deemed important for judging the program's worth or merit. Furthermore, the procedures followed must be technically appropriate, and the conclusions rendered must be connected logically to the data collected. This set of standards is intended to confirm that an evaluation uncovers and communicates accurate information about the program's merit and worth. Six of the twelve Accuracy Standards were considered by Barbara and her teachers to be particularly pertinent to their metaevaluation: Program Documentation, Context Analysis, Described Purposes and Procedures, Valid Information, Justified Conclusions, and Impartial Reporting.

ACCURACY STANDARD 1:
PROGRAM DOCUMENTATION

This standard states that the program being evaluated should be described and documented clearly and accurately so that the program is clearly identified. It is necessary for the evaluator to gain a solid understanding of the program being evaluated, including both the way it was intended to be implemented and the way it actually is implemented (Joint Committee on

Standards for Educational Evaluation, 1994, p. 127). The consultant apparently assumed that the school's intentions for implementation of the Tangerine program were identical with her own. Perhaps she could have demonstrated how the Tangerine procedures were better designed to meet Shannon's student objectives than were the procedures being used. But she failed to do so. As a result, there was inevitably little likelihood that the results of the evaluation would be used.

ACCURACY STANDARD 2:
CONTEXT ANALYSIS

This standard states that the context in which the program exists should be examined in enough detail so that its likely influences on the program can be identified (Joint Committee on Standards for Educational Evaluation, 1994, p. 133). The consultant neglected to obtain contextual information from key players, most notably the principal and the teachers. Information obtained from these sources would probably have led to additional areas of investigation.

ACCURACY STANDARD 3:
DESCRIBED PURPOSES AND PROCEDURES

This standard states that the purposes and procedures of the evaluation should be monitored and described in enough detail so that they can be identified and assessed (Joint Committee on Standards for Educational Evaluation, 1994, p. 137). The evaluator has an obligation to discuss thoroughly and record the client's initial conceptions of the purposes of the evaluation and the intended uses of the findings of the evaluation. As they reviewed the final report of the consultant, Barbara and the teachers found no clear identification of how the procedures used in the evaluation were linked with their purposes. As a result, the consultant's recommendations seemed to have been made on a totally a priori basis.

ACCURACY STANDARD 5:
VALID INFORMATION

Accuracy Standard 5 states that the information-gathering procedures should be chosen or developed and then implemented so that they assure that the interpretation arrived at is valid for the intended use (Joint Committee on Standards for Educational Evaluation, 1994, p. 145). Among other requirements for validity, information-collection procedures must be checked against the objectives and content of the program being evaluated to determine the degree of fit or congruence between them. This check should be informed to some degree both by personnel responsible for implementing the program, as well as by other stakeholders. Clearly this had not been done. In addition, the consultant's reasons for selecting particular procedures and her documentation of evidence that supported the use of each procedure should have been included in a methodology section of the report. This was not done either.

ACCURACY STANDARD 10:
JUSTIFIED CONCLUSIONS

According to this standard, the conclusions reached in an evaluation should be explicitly justified, so that the stakeholders can assess them (Joint Committee on Standards for Educational Evaluation, 1994, p. 177). Supporting data for the consultant's conclusions, at least in terms of the school's objectives for the evaluation, were totally absent from the final report.

ACCURACY STANDARD 11:
IMPARTIAL REPORTING

This standard states that reporting procedures should guard against distortion caused by personal feelings and biases of any party to the evaluation so that evaluation reports fairly reflect the evaluation findings (Joint Committee on Standards for Educational Evaluation, 1994, p. 181). There is a distinct danger whenever an evaluator of a commercial program is also employed by that program. If possible, it is better to use an evaluator who is well-grounded in the intent and implementation of the program, but who is not employed by the program. If this is not possible, clear steps must be taken during the initial stages of contracting for the evaluation to ensure the fairness of all reports.

When Barbara and the Shannon teachers finished their metaevaluation, they felt much wiser about what it takes to perform a competent evaluation and, consequently, much better about what had happened. They would be much better prepared next time and much better consumers of evaluation. Their metaevaluation also made clear to them what it would take to get a comprehensive and useful evaluation for any part of the Shannon educational program.

As she reviewed the work her group had done, Barbara realized that much of the fault for the failed evaluation process had been her own for not being aware of the dangers inherent in the program evaluation process. She was struck also by the fact that most of the problems went back to Propriety Standard 2: Formal Agreements. Her teachers agreed with her that most of the other problems could have been avoided if they had insisted on this early first step. Of course, they also agreed with the obvious point made by a third grade teacher that the formal agreement may have not meant a thing if they had not been aware of the other standards. Clearly the standards were dependent on each other. Applied as a whole, they could guide evaluation into a powerful force for school improvement.

LAYING A FOUNDATION FOR
EFFECTIVE EVALUATION

As you reviewed the thirty Program Evaluation Standards, you may have noticed how closely they parallel good principles of school administration. *Organizational Oversight* (Erlandson, Stark, and Ward, 1996), another volume in the *School Leadership Library*, describes how a foundation for team-building and planning is laid. This foundation is based upon three principles: the maximization of valid information; joint design and control of group tasks; and free and informed choice by all participants. These same principles permeate the Program Evaluation Standards.

If these principles that underlie both organizational and evaluation effectiveness are built into the normal daily operations of the school, including its many evaluation activities, it is much less likely that the principal will be caught off guard by an external evaluation, as Barbara Madison was. A considerable amount of evaluation occurs within the school: evaluation of students through formal testing, grading of assignments, and observations; evaluation of teachers through formal and informal observations and analysis of student achievement; evaluation of curriculum; evaluation of co-curricular activities; and so forth. As we observed, program evaluation includes aggregate measures derived from these evaluations and uses them to evaluate and improve the educational programs which they inform.

As noted earlier, the principal should have a measure of evaluation expertise at both individual and programmatic levels. In addition to the program evaluation expertise that we emphasize in this chapter, the principal must have a firm grasp of the principles of both student evaluation and personnel evaluation. An excellent source book on the purposes and procedures of evaluation is Worthen, Borg, and White's *Measurement and Evaluation in the Schools* (1993), and we strongly suggest that this volume become a part of the principal's professional library. Personnel evaluation is dealt with more specifically in *Staff Development* (Zepeda, 1999), another volume in the *School Leadership Library*. Available also is *The Personnel Evaluation Standards* (Joint Committee on Standards for Educational Evaluation, 1988), which provides a set of standards for personnel evaluation, parallel to those we discussed in this chapter for program evaluation. Both these volumes should also be added to the principal's professional library.

SUMMARY

In this chapter, we have emphasized program evaluation because we believe it provides a strategy for establishing a comprehensive stance toward evaluation at all levels throughout the school. The Joint Committee on Standards for Educational Evaluation expressed a similar view in its succinct statement on the applicability of the Program Evaluation Standards: "Taken as a set, the 30 standards provide a working philosophy for evaluation" (1994, p. xviii). The committee clearly envisioned the standards as the comprehensive approach to evaluation that we portray in this chapter. We believe that systematic application of the principles embodied in the standards will foster a school culture that values valid information and evaluation decisions that are based on it.

ACTION FOLLOW-UP

1. Consider the case of a particular student, with whom you are familiar. (We encourage you to focus on a typical, average student.) Consider all the information that is collected on that student, how it is collected, and how it is applied by the school in making decisions about that student. Now compare these procedures against the Program Evaluation Standards.

   Make a note of what you learn as you proceed through this exercise. Is the total evaluation process truly cognizant of that student's range of needs? Are the results of the evaluations being appropriately directed to the student's needs? Have the procedures used been both efficient and effective? Has the student's dignity and worth been respected throughout the process? Has the evaluation led to useful conclusions and recommendations that will facilitate the continuing educational growth of the student?

2. *The Program Evaluation Standards* (Joint Committee on Standards for Educational Evaluation, 1994) provides considerable specific direction for conducting a metaevaluation, including a Checklist for Applying the Standards. Identify a program evaluation that has been implemented in your school or school district. Using the Program Evaluation Standards, conduct a metaevaluation of that evaluation study. Share your findings with the staff in your school and with other persons who will be responsible for planning and implementing future program evaluations.

3. Identify an educational program in your school that should be evaluated. Plan an evaluation for

that program. Consider each of the program evaluation standards, determining whether or not it is relevant for your evaluation and, if relevant, how it will be met.

4. *The Program Evaluation Standards* provides rich case studies to illustrate application of each of the thirty standards. Form a study group with a few of your colleagues and systematically review each of these case studies and the standards they support. Share with each other how the good and bad practices documented by the case studies have been reflected in your own school experiences. As you do so, consider how program evaluation is affected when it is conducted on a single campus. For instance, in reference to Illustrative Case 1 on pages 155 and 156 of *The Program Evaluation Standards*, how would your efforts to establish reliability for your instruments have been affected if you were focusing on a single school instead of six schools?

3

COLLECTING AND USING INFORMATION

Every school abounds in rich data. These data reflect the many facets of the school, including the building structure and furnishings, the school grounds and the neighborhood, the policies and procedures that guide it, and the many interpersonal activities that occur in it. To a person who had no knowledge about American schools or the way they operate, this overwhelming supply of data would initially be quite bewildering—perhaps as incomprehensible as the religious ceremony of a primitive South American tribe would be to the average American principal.

Data by themselves do not supply meaning, but people can use them to develop meaning. Only when data are structured for a purpose do they yield *information* which the person who observes them can put to useful purposes. A human baby, coming into a bewildering world of sights, sounds, smells, tastes, and tactile sensations, gradually learns to translate these data into usable information; but it takes several years before the child is able to structure a significant amount of data to facilitate efficient two-way communication.

Fortunately, the reader of this book, having operated in schools for extended periods of time in at least two different roles (student and teacher), is likely to already have a relatively efficient system for deriving information from the data that fill the school. For the same reason, nearly all of the school's stakeholders (students, parents, teachers, community members, administrators, school board members) have developed systems for deriving school information and, using this information, have fairly well-defined opinions about how schools operate and how they *ought to* operate.

The problem, however, is that as an individual's information shaping capabilities become more proficient in shaping school data, they are also likely to become less effective. That is, habitual modes of forming opinions and making decisions based on these opinions save considerable time because they use shortcuts for shaping information from the data that surround them. In doing so, however, they typically ignore relevant data that would lead to more accurate usable information.

It often takes a batting coach or a golf professional considerable time to get a batter or golfer to effectively change his or her swing to one that is more effective, and the batter or golfer usually experiences some discomfort in trying to make the necessary adjustment. It is at least as hard for a person in an organizational setting, such as a school, to learn to look for new types of data that will yield more productive information. The longer a person has been a member of an organization, the more likely it is that he or she has found a comfortable way to conveniently obtain satisfactory information and process it in a satisfactory way that yields satisfactory conclusions and decisions. However, *satisfactory* does not mean *optimal*, and over time, as the nature of relevant data changes, the gap between the two grows.

AN EXERCISE IN COLLECTING INFORMATION

We use a hypothetical situation to develop some key principles regarding the collection and use of information in the school. As you proceed through this exercise, take the necessary time to complete the suggested activities. Doing so, and comparing your results with those of colleagues, should provide valuable learning about how you can effectively approach and use the rich supply of information that exists in every school.

A RARE OPPORTUNITY

After going through a round of interviews, you have been offered the position of principal in one of your state's premier schools at a considerable increase in salary. The school is in a part of the state in which you have always wanted to live. You are flattered and intrigued by the offer, but you feel that you would like to know more about the school, the population it serves, and its potential for educational excellence before you commit yourself. The superintendent, the school board, and the current principal (who is retiring) are so convinced that you are the person for the job that they make you a truly unusual offer. They invite you to spend a week at the school, just finding out what you feel you need to know about the school. Everything in the school will be open to you. You can look through any files; observe classes; attend meetings; conduct interviews with students, teachers, parents, and administrators; and obtain any other information that you consider necessary.

Because the school will be in session during the time of your own spring break, you decide to accept this offer to find out more about the school. At first, it seems as though a week will be more than enough time to find out what you'd like to know about the school. However, as you begin itemizing the information you'd like to obtain, you realize that you will have to schedule your time quite carefully.

As a first step in planning the week, you put together a simple table to help you organize your quest. The table organizes your information search around two simple questions:

♦ What information are you seeking?

♦ How can you obtain it?

The table that you constructed is shown in Figure 3.1. A possible first entry is provided for your guidance. Before reading further in the text, complete this table to guide your data collection in the new school. If possible, share your results with colleagues and compare your answers with theirs.

A REVIEW OF YOUR INFORMATION COLLECTION PLANS

Look over the information that you are going to seek and the way you plan to obtain it. Ask yourself these questions:

♦ What documents, records, and other artifacts will you seek? (For example: standardized test scores, meeting agenda, teacher grades, course syllabi, student portfolios.)

FIGURE 3.1. ORGANIZING FOR INFORMATION COLLECTION

Information Sought	Method for Obtaining Information
Teaching methods used by faculty	Classroom observations Review of lesson plans and teaching units Teacher interviews

- ◆ What information will you get through direct observation? (For example: observations of classrooms, meetings, athletic events.)
- ◆ What information will you get through interviews and questionnaires? (For example: one-on-one interviews with teachers, students, parents, administrators; group interviews; teacher questionnaires.)

These three groups of information sources may be contrasted in terms of their *reactivity* to you as the information seeker. The first group of sources (documents, records, and other artifacts) were created for other purposes, independent of your visit to the school, and will not be shaped or disturbed by your presence. We might say that they have *no reactivity* to you.

By contrast, sources in the second group are affected by your presence and, therefore, may be considered to be *more reactive*. As a result, the impact of your presence on the observation will, to some degree, affect what you are able to observe. Your behavior as an observer can increase or decrease the reactivity of the observation. For instance, in a classroom observation, if you are feverishly making notes (or even tape recording the class), there is likely to be a high degree of reactivity. The problem here, of course, is that you can't be sure just how the class has been affected by your presence or if it would have been significantly different if you weren't there. At the other extreme, you may go to a school football game and sit quietly in the stands as you make mental notes about the attitudes and behavior of the student body and, in so doing, have little impact on what you observe. The behavior of the observer must balance the importance of the information that can potentially be gained through careful systematic observation with the danger of distorting information through obtrusive observation.

The third group of information sources (interviews and questionnaires) is potentially even more intrusive, and, therefore, likely to produce *high degrees of reactivity*. By their very nature, the interview and questionnaire interject information into the setting that will change it in some way; the challenge is to not change it in a way that will distort the response. Considerations similar to those that apply to observations, also apply here. On the one hand, you will want the questions that you use in an interview or questionnaire to get information that is as precise as possible and that directly addresses your identified needs. On the other hand, there is always the concern that you may not know precisely what information you need, and that you may have to use open ended questions on a questionnaire or guide a more rambling conversation in order to allow your respondents, who are the experts on their own school, to share the full range and depth of the relevant information they possess. You will need to make decisions like these as you prepare for using interviews and questionnaires.

The same three groups of information sources may also be viewed in terms of their flexibility in fitting into your schedule. Prior to spending your week at the school you will need to make plans for *when* you will get the desired information. The first group (documents, records, and artifacts) is the most flexible. Those documents and records that can be copied can be put into your briefcase for analysis in the evenings or after you've returned home. It is very likely that a secretary can copy the materials for you and thus save you even this minimal time in collecting this information. Even items that must remain in the school can often be examined after the school day is over and usually at odd hours or half hours during the school day. By contrast, planned observations are generally the least flexible. The algebra class, the school assembly, and the faculty meeting will have fixed places on your calendar if you choose to observe them. Interviews and questionnaires are more flexible in this regard, but they also must be coordinated with the availability of the people you wish to include in your data collection. Scheduling decisions should be completed as much as possible before you begin your week in residence at the school.

SCHEDULING INFORMATION COLLECTION

Scheduling information collection, then, is your next task. Now that you know what you're looking for and how you can obtain it, how will you structure your week to make best use of the time? Make a calendar similar to the one shown in Figure 3.2 to schedule your week's information collection activities.

After you've completed your information collection schedule, ask yourself these questions:

♦ Why did you decide to collect certain pieces of information at certain times?

♦ How are you planning for your earlier information collection activities to help structure your later information collection activities?

FIGURE 3.2. INFORMATION COLLECTION CALENDAR

	Monday	Tuesday	Wednesday	Thursday	Friday
Early Morning					
8 a.m.					
9 a.m.					
10 a.m.					
11 a.m.					
12 p.m.					
1 p.m.					
2 p.m.					
3 p.m.					
4 p.m.					
After School					

Once again, if possible, compare your answers with those of colleagues.

A REVIEW OF YOUR INFORMATION-COLLECTION SCHEDULE

While there may be no one best way to schedule your proposed information collection, there are several principles you should have kept in mind:

♦ Go from the general to the specific.

At the beginning of the week you know the least about the school that you will know all week. You also know the least about what you need to know. Therefore, you should begin the week by seeking information that will structure your subsequent information collection activity. To do this, you can use your knowledge about schools generally to ask questions that set patterns for the remainder of your search. Ask to see a summary of student standardized test scores, including any available breakdowns of scores by socioeconomic and ethnic groups. Ask to see a summary of the professional staff that shows degrees, number of years at the school, and total years experience. In the same way, you may wish to take a tour of the neighborhoods that send students to the school. Take a tour of the building. All the while, make quick notes in a pocket notebook that will lead to more specific inquiry in the days that follow. Use the information you gather in these ways to plan more specific data gathering efforts.

♦ Start with nonreactive information collection strategies.

There are two reasons to start with nonreactive strategies. The first of these is closely related to the first principle of moving from the general to the specific. As noted in the suggestions made in regard to that principle, many of these nonreactive strategies tend to provide good context for formulating subsequent questions. In addition, close attention to information provided by these nonreactive strategies can help to diminish the negative consequences of subsequent strategies that tend to be more reactive. For instance, by better understanding the faculty's background and experience, you may be able to structure a questionnaire that will neither confuse nor insult them. You may learn about sensitive areas in the school and how better to ask questions about them in interviews. You may also learn how to avoid subtle cultural taboos that can shipwreck your entire mission.

♦ Analyze your data as you proceed.

Use any available time in the week to review the data you've collected, to make interpretations from them, and to structure your future data gathering efforts. Certain questions that you had before you arrived at the school will be refined through this process and new questions will be formed. As your understanding of the school increases, you can use this to focus your inquiry and your subsequent evaluation efforts. Much of Friday should be devoted to collecting the most important data you will need to complete your analysis of the school.

♦ Schedule flexibility.

Not everything will go just as you planned for it to go. There will be cancellations of appointments, and unanticipated opportunities will arise. Lay out blocks of time in your schedule, particularly after the first two days of your visit, that can be allocated to observation and interview opportunities that become available after your visit has begun. Many of these opportunities, or their comparative value, will not be known to you prior to your arrival at the school. As suggested earlier, Friday, particularly, should have major blocks of flexible time that will enable you to make last minute data collection decisions as you bring your visit to a close.

♦ Protect opportunity time.

A specific way of building flexibility into your schedule is by protecting opportunity time. You know enough about schools from your past experience to recognize that certain times of the day and week will afford rich opportunity for collecting information from a variety of sources. For instance, you know that times right after the end of the school day may be particularly good for catching busy teachers or administrators long enough to ask one or two key questions. You know also that this is a time when small-group teacher and administrator meetings that you would like to observe may be scheduled at the last minute. You can check in advance with the principal of the school to find out what other times are likely to provide last-minute opportunities to collect information. These will differ from school to school. Once you've identified these opportunity times, don't schedule them for retrieving documents or for engaging in other events that could just as easily be scheduled at times that are less opportunity rich.

A CHANGE IN SCHEDULE

Let's assume that after you have made your plans for spending a week at the new school your situation at home changes, which means that you will only be able to devote Monday of your vacation week to your on-site information gathering junket. What will you do now? You could throw up your hands and call the situation impossible; but remember that this one day of learning about the school, which is at your convenience, is more than most prospective principals get. Consider how you will spend your time that day. What types of information will you collect? How and when will you collect it?

Review the five principles that we identified:

+ Go from the general to the specific.
+ Start with nonreactive information collection strategies.
+ Analyze your data as you proceed.
+ Schedule flexibility.
+ Protect *opportunity time.*

These principles apply to your new situation even though the time allocated to the task has been drastically shortened. Make out a tentative schedule for collecting information as if you only have Monday to spend at the new school. Once again, if possible, compare your answers with those of your colleagues.

REVIEWING YOUR ONE-DAY SCHEDULE

The first two principles suggest that you should go from the general to the specific and that you start with nonreactive strategies. There are many types of broad information that you can obtain from the new school in a nonreactive way prior to your ever setting foot in the school. The current principal of the school can send you summaries of test scores, grades, class schedules, teaching units, lesson plans, and so forth that will provide you with much background about the school. He can also send you copies of local newspapers and other documents that will tell you much about the community. You might, at least on some relatively nonreactive topics, ask the current principal to distribute a brief questionnaire prior to your arrival. Use this information to learn about the school and to schedule your limited time for the single day. You might even consider arriving in town during the preceding weekend in order to get a feel for the community and the people who live in it. You can also begin your analysis of the information that you obtain before you arrive and make some tentative interpretations of the situation that you can test when you get to the school.

Then, using the principles of building-in flexible time and protecting time to take advantage of unanticipated opportunities, schedule some specific interviews and observations for the morning, perhaps some even before school begins. Because your time is limited, you will want to choose your interviews and observations carefully. Interviews, because they can be more easily shaped to garner specific information, are generally more efficient than observations, and you will probably want to allocate more of your limited time to them. In selecting respondents for interviews, be careful to identify individuals who are likely to present you with the richest information (e.g., grade-level or department chairs, the head secretary, senior teachers), but during these interviews, be alert for other voices and minority views. If you can identify these other sources during the morning, try to schedule them for the afternoon. Keeping in mind the principle of analyzing as you go along, try to schedule some time alone during the late morning or at lunch to review what you've learned and to plan specifically for the afternoon. Finally, knowing that you will have many questions when you get back home, exchange phone, e-mail, and fax numbers with the office staff and with key individuals so that you can continue to improve your understanding of the school as you try to refine your understanding and come to a conclusion in the days that follow.

LEARNING FROM THE INFORMATION-COLLECTION EXERCISE

The exercise that you just completed does not represent a situation that will occur very often in your career. Nevertheless, there is much that you can learn from it that will serve you well as the principal of any school. In the exercise, you collected information and used it to learn about a school in order to facilitate a very important decision that you would have to make about it. In this respect, the exercise was very much like what you will need to do as a principal. The principal must be able to identify needed information and then use that information to facilitate action.

Herbert Simon (1977) identified four phases of activity in a managerial decision model:

- *Intelligence activity*, which consists of searching the environment for occasions (problems) calling for decisions;

- *Design activity*, which centers on inventing, developing, and analyzing possible courses of action;

- *Choice activity*, which encompasses the actual selection of a particular course of action from those available; and

- *Review activity*, which consists of evaluating past choices.

In an overall sense, this week (or day) of information collection focused on the first phase. However, when seen as a total activity, all four phases of the managerial decision model were represented in it. Its purpose was to shape alternative courses of action for yourself: accept the position; reject the position; or stipulate conditions that must be met for you to accept the position. This will lead, within a fairly short period of time, to your decision about the position, which, in turn, will establish an information and decision sequence that you will want to revisit to improve your future decisions in your new position as principal of the school, or in looking at other professional opportunities.

However, even within the week, the four phases of the Simon model were in operation. Your first efforts were in the intelligence phase and helped you to understand the overall environment of the school, and to learn what you needed to know and how to best obtain that needed information. From here you used your scheduled information-collection strategies, your continuing analysis, and your protected opportunity time to design, develop, and choose subsequent information-collection strategies. Throughout the week you evaluated how well your information-collection strategies were working so that you could make your subsequent activities more effective.

These patterns for collecting information and shaping it for decisions will serve a principal in all aspects of school activity. The principal will always be faced with questions such as:

+ What do I need to know about the school?
+ Where can I obtain the necessary information to tell me what I need to know?
+ How can this information be used to facilitate my decisions?
+ How can my decision making activity be used to improve future decisions?

What you've done in this exercise may have no direct application to your career, but the pattern of considering the range of data that is available in the school and using it to make decisions should be replicated every day on the job.

SUMMARY

In this chapter, we considered the broad range of data that abound in the school and the context (neighborhood, school district, etc.) in which the school operates. We also considered the different types of school data that are available to the principal, the different strategies that may be used to collect that data, and the different information uses to which that data may be put.

We also examined how different information-collection strategies can be combined, and how they can support each other in serving the information needs of the principal. We saw how data can be collected to inform original questions formulated by the principal, and how data can be used to refine subsequent questions and information-collection strategies. We saw, in terms of Simon's management decision model, how the principal can systematically be engaged in information collection as an intelligence activity, a design activity, a choice activity, and a review activity to enhance information-driven decisions throughout the school organization.

ACTION FOLLOW-UP

1. If you are currently a principal, ask yourself the question: *What significant problems exist in my school that I don't have solutions for?* (Another way of asking this question might be: *What school problems are keeping me awake at night?*) Then map out an information collection schedule that is designed to identify a solution for each of these problems.

   If you are not currently a principal, work collaboratively with a principal to ask these same questions and to develop an information collection schedule that addresses them.

2. Implement (or work with the principal to implement) the information collection schedule, and develop solutions to the problems you have identified.

3. Develop an information collection schedule for monitoring each solution as it is implemented.

4

STRUCTURING AND SCHEDULING PROGRAM EVALUATION

In Chapter 2, we defined program evaluation, considered the importance of program evaluation for the operation of the school, and examined the standards against which a program evaluation may be assessed to determine both its technical and ethical adequacy. Evaluation, as Scriven (1991) noted, is the process by which the merit, worth, and value of things are determined. By ascertaining and ascribing value to what happens in the various parts of its educational program, the school obtains direction for the critical choices it makes in determining the goals, resources, and procedures that will be used to guide and implement the program. We also examined in some depth the standards of utility, feasibility, propriety, and accuracy against which a program evaluation may be judged, and we then considered a practical example for making such judgments.

In Chapter 3, we considered some principles that the principal should keep in mind for collecting and using information to support program evaluation in his or her school. We also provided a practical exercise in applying these principles.

In this chapter, we consider how a principal may plan for and structure program evaluation, how a principal may schedule evaluations of the various elements of the school's total educational program, and how these elements can be effectively related within the constraints of the school year.

DETERMINING A FOCUS FOR
PROGRAM EVALUATION

As a first step in structuring and scheduling program evaluation for the school, we suggest that the principal take time to determine the focus of the evaluation. The principal might begin by asking a series of basic questions:

♦ What should be evaluated? (Why should it be evaluated?)

♦ How should it be evaluated?

♦ What will be done with the results of the evaluation?

Consider the first question: *What should be evaluated*? At first, this question may seem patently obvious. The principal may respond simply by listing *programs* that operate in the school: the mathematics program, the reading program, the student activities program, and so forth. But consider these questions more closely. What will it mean to evaluate the mathematics program. Are we concerned with student achievement? With the adequacy of mathematics materials? With the instructional excellence of mathematics instruction as demonstrated by teachers? Or are we concerned with all these things and more? Or, suppose that we take just one of the possibilities: student achievement. What does this mean? Does it mean performance on the state minimum competency test or on teacher-made tests? Does it mean a demonstrated desire and ability on the part of students to take advanced mathematics courses in the future? Hopefully, you are beginning to see (if you hadn't already seen it) that the question about what should be evaluated is not a simple one.

This first basic question, about what should be evaluated, can be further refined by a supplemental question: *Why should it be evaluated*? Some answers to this are indeed obvious. For instance, if there is a state-mandated test in place, this is both a necessary and sufficient reason for doing it. However, it may not be complete. The principal should want to know how well an educational program is functioning for the simple reason that the principal needs to know how the students in the school may optimally benefit from it. What can we learn from the state mathematics competency test that will provide direction for enhancing students' ability in mathematics and help us adjust our curriculum and instruction to meet their needs?

How should it be evaluated? Once we determine what we want evaluated, we need to consider how it needs to be evaluated. Does the state competency test tell us everything we need to know? How can it be supplemented by teacher-made tests, by standardized norm-referenced tests, by diagnostic tests, by teacher and/or student attitude surveys, by follow-up studies? Because resources of time, money, and energy for evaluating are always limited, we need to consider how, within the limits we have, can we obtain sufficient information to answer our basic question.

Finally, we need to ask, *What will be done with the results of the evaluation?* Every principal knows that there are evaluations of various types in schools that are never used for any educational purpose at all, or that, at best, are used for very limited purposes. Some of these are imposed from the outside (and the principal may have little power to control them), but some are initiated from within the school. Consider for example, the time that is spent by teachers, particularly at the high school level, in developing and administering final examinations. Typically, the results are used primarily to assign a grade for the course that has just been completed. Although much valuable information may be learned about a student's achievement, little is done with the examination to determine how that student's needs will be met in the future. Unfortunately, this is often true for other examinations given during the year. Time, energy, and materials are too valuable to spend on evaluation that is not going to be used to advance the educational program. Before initiating an evaluation, the principal should have a clear idea of what will be done with the results of the evaluation.

SOME ALTERNATIVE APPROACHES
TO PROGRAM EVALUATION

As we noted in Chapter 2, different stakeholders will have different interests in the conduct of an evaluation, and, accordingly, how an evaluation is structured will provide different types of information that serve different stakeholder needs. Worthen and Sanders (1987) have provided an analysis of six different approaches to evaluation:

♦ Objectives-oriented;

♦ Management-oriented;

♦ Consumer-oriented;

♦ Expertise-oriented;

♦ Adversary-oriented; and

♦ Naturalistic and participant-oriented.

Each of these evaluation approaches has somewhat different purposes, characteristics, and uses, and each makes different contributions to program evaluation.

OBJECTIVES-ORIENTED APPROACH

The *objectives-oriented* approach was developed in the 1930s, notably during the Eight-Year Study (Smith and Tyler, 1941) and was further articulated by Ralph Tyler in the years that followed. (See, for example, Tyler, R. W. (1950). *Basic Principles of Curriculum and Instruction*.) The names of its major proponents and developers (e.g., Popham, Mager, Cronbach, Bloom, and Krathwohl) are familiar to educators who have been involved in curriculum development and evaluation. From this approach have emanated the behavioral objectives movement and also the widespread emphasis on criterion-referenced testing, as exemplified by the National Assessment of Educational Progress and various statewide testing programs.

One clear benefit of the behavioral objectives approach has been that it has forced educators to consider what specifically they want to accomplish and to clarify it through unambiguous language. As the approach has developed and as resources have been invested in it, test and measurement practices have clearly improved.

The approach has also come under considerable criticism. Many observers feel that it does not provide a basis for distinguishing between the value of competing objectives, that it may ignore important outcomes that are not specified in the program objectives, that it ignores the context in which the goals are being pursued, and that, by prespecifying objectives, it promotes an inflexible approach to evaluation that does not accommodate changing circumstances.

MANAGEMENT-ORIENTED APPROACH

The *management-oriented* evaluation approach is exemplified by the CIPP model of Daniel Stufflebeam (Stufflebeam et al., 1971). The clear purpose of the approach is to serve the needs of decision-makers, those persons who are given the responsibility for administering a program. Obviously, this approach has great relevance for the principal.

CIPP is an acronym for four different kinds of decisions that are needed in the implementation of an educational program. *C* stands for *Context Evaluation*. Context evaluation serves *planning decisions* that must be made in an educational program. These decisions focus directly on the definition of the objectives that will guide the program. *I* stands for *Input Evaluation*. Input Evaluation serves *structuring decisions* about what resources (procedures, personnel, budget, schedule, facilities, etc.) should be allocated to a program, what strategies should be used for applying those resources, and what plan should guide the implementation of the program. *P* stands for *Process Evaluation*. Process evaluation serves *implementing decisions*. These are the decisions that are based upon what is actually happening as the program is being implemented. Process evaluation asks: How well is the program functioning? What barriers to implementation are being encountered? What revisions should be made? As these questions are answered, decisions can be made to monitor, control, and refine the process. The second *P* refers to *Product Evaluation*. Product Evaluation serves *recycling decisions* that are based upon answers to questions such as: What are the accomplishments of the program? How can what we learned from the evaluation be used to reshape the educational program? Recycling decisions are made to continue, improve, modify, or terminate an educational program. In addition to serving recycling decisions during the course of an evaluation, they also form the foundation for the context evaluation that will guide the next cycle of program evaluation.

Figure 4.1 is a 2×2 matrix that shows graphically how the four types of evaluations identified by the CIPP model and the four types of decisions they serve are related to each other and to the total process of program evaluation. Decisions may be classified by whether they pertain to *ends* or *means*, as shown by the headings for the two rows on the figure. They can also be classified by how they pertain to *intentions* or *actualities,* as shown by the headings of the two columns. Although the actual process of education is never completely linear, we may follow the logical flow of the model if we start in the upper-left quadrant (context evaluation—planning decisions) and proceed in a counterclockwise direction through the model. Recycling decisions (upper-right quadrant) lead back to a reformulation of objectives.

FIGURE 4.1. THE CIPP MODEL: EVALUATION AND DECISION

	Intended	Actual
Ends	**Context Evaluation** serves **PLANNING DECISIONS** to determine objectives	**Product Evaluation** serves **RECYCLING DECISIONS** to judge and react to attainments
Means	**Input Evaluation** serves **STRUCTURING DECISIONS** to design procedures	**Process Evaluation** serves **IMPLEMENTING DECISIONS** to utilize, control, and refine procedures

Source: Adapted from Stufflebeam, D.L., W.J. Foley, W.J. Gephart, E.G. Guba, R.L. Hammond, H.O. Merriman, and M.M. Provus. (1971). *Educational Evaluation and Decision Making.* Itasca, Ill.: F.E. Peacock Publishers.

As Worthen and Sanders (1987) note regarding the management-oriented evaluation approach: "Perhaps its greatest strength is that it gives focus to the evaluation" (p. 83). Decisions must be made by busy administrators, and they simply don't have the time to collect large amounts of information that may or may not prove useful in making decisions. They need to incorporate efficiency into the decision making process. The management-oriented approach has also pointed out the value of midcourse corrections when evidence warrants that they are needed. Principals cannot afford to allow a substandard program to run its course simply because an initial decision was made to implement a program. The approach clarifies the range of decisions that a principal, or other school administrator, must make and gives direction about their effective application.

If providing focus is the major strength of the management-oriented approach, it also suggests its major weakness: the danger of failing to recognize critical issues that lie outside the administrator's focus. Although the management-oriented approach provides invaluable evaluation tools for program evaluation in the school, the principal needs to supplement it with other approaches to avoid being sabotaged by those inevitable blind spots that go with the hectic, energy-draining job of the principal.

CONSUMER-ORIENTED APPROACH

As the name suggests, the *consumer-oriented* approach to program evaluation is designed to serve the needs of those who purchase educational products. A wide definition is used for educational products and includes "curriculum packages, workshops, instructional media, in-service training opportunities, staff evaluation, forms or procedures, new technology, software and equipment, educational materials and supplies, and even services to schools." (Worthen and Sanders, 1987, p. 87) As more and more money has gone into education and as the products used in education have become more technical and voluminous, the danger of purchasing a substandard product has increased. As a result, the need for this type of evaluation has grown. A major contributor to the consumer-oriented approach was Michael Scriven, who both established criteria for evaluating educational products (Scriven, 1967) and published a checklist (Scriven, 1974) for making decisions about educational products. Other checklists and systems for evaluating educational products have also become available. Notable in this regard is the Educational Products Information Exchange (EPIE) that has published a newsletter (*EPIE Forum*) that furnishes evaluative information to potential consumers much in the manner of the *Consumer Reports*, published by the Consumers Union.

The benefits provided by the various consumer-oriented evaluation approaches are obvious and have virtually become a necessity in this age when so many educational products, of diverse types, are being used by schools and when so many vendors are competing for the available dollars of educational institutions. The principal will do well to make him- or herself aware of the literature available on this approach, if for no other reason than to provide good stewardship of the public funds with which he or she has been entrusted.

EXPERTISE-ORIENTED APPROACH

Older even than the objectives-oriented approach that has dominated educational evaluation since the 1930s is the *expertise-oriented* evaluation approach. Worthen and Sanders (1987) have identified some leading examples of this time honored approach: "doctoral oral examinations, proposal review panels, professional reviews conducted by professional accreditation bodies, reviews of institutions or individuals by state or national licensing agencies, reviews of educators' performance for decisions concerning promotion or tenure, peer reviews of articles submitted to 'refereed' professional journals, site visits of educational programs conducted at the behest of the program's sponsor, reviews and recommendations of prestigious 'blue-ribbon' panels, and even the critique offered by the ubiquitous expert who exists, at least one to every educational system, and whose *raison d'etre* is to serve in a self-appointed watchdog role" (pp. 98–99). Worthen and Sanders (p. 99) organize these diverse examples into four categories:

- Formal professional review systems;
- Informal professional review systems;
- Ad hoc panel reviews; and
- Ad hoc individual reviews.

Although principals have knowledge of such expertise-oriented evaluations and have participated in them as well, most will not see major uses for them in their own program evaluations. They should keep in mind that these evaluations are used in their schools (e.g., cheerleader or football tryouts), and for some purposes such evaluations may usefully be extended to other areas.

ADVERSARY-ORIENTED APPROACH

Bias is always a danger in evaluation, and most evaluation approaches make at least a tacit assumption that the evaluator will be impartial in conducting the evaluation. Yet experience shows that this is very difficult to achieve, particularly when the stakes are high and/or when emotions are involved. Every experienced principal knows of situations when one group of very sincere and competent teachers has urged the adoption of one course of action while, at the same time, another group of sincere and competent teachers has urged adoption of another course. A few principals have learned how to use this opposed expertise to facilitate productive decisions. This process is at the heart of what Worthen and Sanders identify as the *adversary-oriented* evaluation approach.

Instead of trying to avoid bias, adversary-oriented evaluations attempt to balance it, allowing advocates on the different sides of a controversial issue to make the case for their respective positions. If this approach sounds unscientific, keep in mind that it is not without precedent in our society. This is exactly what judges and juries do in deciding extremely important legal issues. Major social questions are not solved very readily by the scientific method. These problems are holistic and complex and are inevitably wrapped in a web of personal motives and interpersonal relations that are impossible to treat as discrete variables that can be dispassionately manipulated or analyzed. Used appropriately, adversary-oriented approaches may help the principal with some extremely difficult problems that face the school. They may be used not only to look at the merits of two opposing views but may also be used to examine the relative merits of several alternative views.

The adversary-oriented approach is not without danger. First, it does no good to present different points of view on a matter if the judge or jury who will decide the matter is biased and has, in fact, already decided that one side has the superior case. Thus it becomes extremely important not only that opposing views are given full opportunity to be heard but that the person(s) who will make the judgment are both competent and unbiased. It may at times be useful for an unbiased expert to be brought in from the outside to decide the case. However, we have been impressed by a handful of principals who themselves have served as judge and used adversary debates to render high-quality decisions for difficult problems.

Principals who would use this method to make important decisions ought first to examine themselves to see if they are really prepared to do it. First, they need to ask themselves if they have the background to render a competent judgment in the area being considered. If not, they need to either abandon the method or find a competent judge. Second, they need to ask themselves if they've already made up their minds about the issue at hand. If they have, they should abandon the thought of using the procedure. The school will be better served if they simply make the decision they have arrived at, even if it appears autocratic (which it probably is). Third, they need to ask if their teachers, parents, and other stakeholders have sufficient confidence in them to make competent, unbiased decisions. Unlike the judge at a court of law, who can make a legal decision and then go his own way, the principal will also be around to implement the decision.

NATURALISTIC AND PARTICIPANT-ORIENTED APPROACH

Naturalistic and participant-oriented evaluation approaches have arisen in recent decades in reaction to what were perceived as overly mechanistic approaches that overlooked the really important, human issues in education in favor of isolated bits of objective evidence that supports fragmented behavioral objectives. The early work of Robert Stake (1967) in developing *The Countenance of Educational Evaluation*, as well as his later work in promoting responsive evaluation (1975) and the case study method (1978), and the work of Guba and Lincoln (1981, 1989) in the development of the constructivist inquiry paradigm, have brought naturalistic and participant-oriented evaluation into the foreground as a legitimate approach.

Because of its holistic approach to context-bound human organizational problems, the naturalistic approach is particularly well-suited to answering the really difficult questions that are unique to a particular school campus. By reframing the situation in new ways that are responsive to the understandings and meanings held by the school's various stakeholders, this approach may enable productive decisions regarding those troublesome interpersonal issues of the school that are literally keeping the principal awake at night.

Because of its emphasis upon a particular social context, such as a school, naturalistic evaluation avoids excessive reliance upon precise quantitative measurement by standardized instruments in making judgments about educational programs. It openly questions whether objectivity is possible or whether it is even a useful goal.

As a result, critics of this approach have suggested that such evaluation, particularly in the hands of a novice, may be sloppy and biased. These criticisms are valid, but they are also valid for any of the evaluation approaches we have considered. The evaluator can take the necessary steps, usefully described by Guba and Lincoln (1989) and Erlandson, Harris, Skipper, and Allen (1993), to ensure that neither sloppiness nor bias destroys the value of the evaluation.

Critics have also maintained that naturalistic approaches are too complex and cumbersome and, as a result, take too much time and are too expensive. This is another valid concern, but a significant amount of time devoted to understanding and responding to overwhelming problem areas may be a bargain for the principal. Furthermore, it is not clear that, at least in the hands of a professional who has received training in naturalistic research, the inquiry and evaluation processes are any more time-consuming and expensive than those associated with what might be considered more traditional approaches. The principal would do well to become more familiar with this mode of understanding his or her school.

Once again, we encourage principals to find out more about these alternative educational approaches. Each can make real contributions to evaluation of the total school program, and the principal should know when and how to use them. Each also has its own particular benefits and limitations. It is well worth the principal's time to consider what each of these approaches has to offer, and we would encourage you to investigate each of them more, either by reading the fuller descriptions provided by Worthen and Sanders or, even better, by going to the works of the proponents of the various approaches.

We turn now to the steps that a principal may take to organize evaluation of the educational program in his or her school.

BUILDING A PLAN FOR PROGRAM EVALUATION

The principal may begin to build a plan for program evaluation by returning to the basic questions with which we began this chapter:

- What should be evaluated? (Why should it be evaluated?)
- How should it be evaluated?
- What will be done with the results of the evaluation?

WHAT SHOULD BE EVALUATED?

The first question, *What should be evaluated?* (and its related subquestion: *Why should it be evaluated?*), provides basic direction for evaluation by focusing attention on the critical elements of the educational program. For purposes of illustration, we focus on one major program that is common to all schools, the reading program. What do we need to know about the reading program? As suggested above, this question may be most efficiently served by asking: Why are we concerned about evaluating the reading program?

Let's list a few of the reasons why we are concerned about the success of the reading program:

- Reading is a basic skill that the school is expected to develop in all students.

- Reading is foundational to mastery of nearly all other school subjects.
- Reading is a key to success in future educational experiences and the world of work.
- Reading opens a window on the wonder and excitement of the universe.

These reasons suggest a number of things that we may want to learn from our evaluation:

- Are our students meeting the state's and the community's expectations for reading achievement?
- To what degree are all students meeting success in acquiring reading skills?
- How well are students able to handle reading assignments in their other school subjects?
- How well do students perform at the next levels of their educational experience?
- How well do high school graduates meet employer's expectations for reading ability?
- How much enjoyment do students get out of reading?
- How much reading do students do on their own initiative?
- What do students choose to read?

We could probably add others.

It does not necessarily follow, just because we recognize these reasons for students to acquire reading skills, that we will necessarily evaluate all of them directly. We cannot say for certain, just because students score high on standardized reading tests, that they will have sufficient reading skills for success in their next level of education. But there is a very strong positive correlation, and we may not need to make a check on their ability to handle the reading at advanced levels of public school or higher education. Similarly, we may not need to independently evaluate their ability to handle their reading assignments in other school subjects, but we probably need to be sensitive to teachers' reports of difficulties that they encounter. On the other hand, reading skill, as measured by many standardized tests, may be positively correlated with enjoyment of reading and wide taste in reading, but we also know that many students with adequate reading skills don't enjoy reading very much and don't use reading as an active tool to satisfy their thirst for knowledge. We may wish to incorporate regular processes to give us some insight on the reading habits of students if we believe they are important.

How Should It Be Evaluated?

We might begin to answer this question about the reading program by first listing the elements of the reading program that we believe that we need to evaluate:

- ◆ Basic reading skill for all students.
- ◆ Success in later schooling and the workplace.
- ◆ Success in other school subjects.
- ◆ Wonder and excitement about reading.

For each of these elements we can list the major ways we will seek to evaluate them:

- ◆ Basic reading skill for all students:
  - • Use statewide minimum competency tests.
  - • Disaggregate scores by classroom, by race, and by ethnicity.
  - • Do follow-up diagnostic testing of individual students.
- ◆ Success in later schooling and the workplace:
  - • Use statewide minimum competency tests.
  - • Use norm-referenced test.
- ◆ Success in other subjects:
  - • Check with classroom teachers regarding students' ability to handle written materials in various curricular areas.
- ◆ Wonder and excitement about reading:
  - • Check with classroom teachers and librarian concerning student reading habits.

WHAT WILL BE DONE WITH THE RESULTS OF THE EVALUATION?

This basic question may be divided into two types of things that should be done with the results: (1) the results of the evaluation should be used to *strengthen the educational program;* (2) the results should be used to *improve the evaluation plan.* To determine how the results of the evaluation may be used to strengthen the reading program, another series of questions may be asked. For example:

♦ Is the curriculum in line with the school's reading goals?

If not, make necessary changes. Where particular classes fall short, provide support to bring instruction into line with those goals.

♦ Are students successful in later schooling and the workplace?

Check with administrators and teachers at next level of schooling. Conduct follow-up studies of graduates. Try to identify any changes that need to be made in the reading program.

♦ Are students successful with reading materials in other subjects?

If there is evidence that they are having difficulty, consider working on particular reading skills that are lacking or possibly selecting other textbooks.

A single question, regarding each of our goals for the reading program, may be asked to determine how we might improve the evaluation plan:

♦ Are current tests and other evaluation procedures telling us what we need to know?

If they are fully telling us what we feel we need to know about each of the elements of the school's reading program, we need to consider how we might augment, modify, or otherwise change what we are doing. If not, we need to consider changing our tests.

What we have described about developing an evaluation plan for a school reading program is summarized in Figure 4.2. Note the first column headed *What should be evaluated?* Under this column we have identified proposed outcomes of the reading program that relate to the four principal reasons we feel we need to evaluate the reading program. In the next column (*How should it be evaluated?*) we list typical and available measures that we can use to obtain information on each of the proposed outcomes. In the third column (*How will the results of the evaluation be used?*) are listed potential applications of the information we have collected. The development of a simple chart such as this is a good first step in building a plan for program evaluation. A total evaluation plan for the school, including the various parts of the school's total educational program (e.g., mathematics program, student activities program, guidance program, athletic program, etc.) may be built in the same way.

COLLECTING AND ANALYZING INFORMATION FOR A COMPREHENSIVE PROGRAM EVALUATION

It should be clear to the reader that we see program evaluation as a major aspect of the principal's job. It should also be clear that it will be a very time- and energy-consuming part of the job. In fact, it may seem that if the principal asks the questions and goes through the steps that we illustrated for a reading program, and recommended for all elements of a school's educational program, that the job will be overwhelming. In a sense this is true. What we have proposed here about program evaluation is, in fact, the principal's job, which has truly become an overwhelming one. However, although the principal has responsibility for program evaluation in his or her school, he or she should not try to do it alone. Many people in the school have contributions to make, and the principal must enlist their help in building the plan. After all, teachers, counselors, and other school professionals should have at least as much ownership in the educational program as the principal. Their active involvement in an evaluation plan that makes a difference in the educational program is a key factor in building this sense of ownership.

FIGURE 4.2. AN EVALUATION PLAN FOR A MIDDLE SCHOOL READING PROGRAM

What should be evaluated?	How should it be evaluated?	Potential applications of the evaluation (How will results of the evaluation be used?)
Basic reading skill of all middle school students.	Statewide minimum competency tests. Disaggregate scores by classroom, race, and ethnicity. Followup diagnostic testing of individual students.	Alignment of curriculum with objectives of statewide competency tests. Application of different instructional strategies for different groups. Design of particular strategies for particular students.
Success in later schooling and the workplace.	Norm-referenced tests. Check with high school administrators on reading performance of freshman class.	Evaluate adequacy of norm referenced tests currently in use. Alignment of curriculum with legitimate norm-referenced objectives and reading requirements for performance in high school.
Success in all subjects.	Check on reading expectations and reading performance in all subjects.	Train all subject area teachers to be reading teachers in their own specialties. Teach reading skills for particular subject areas. Change adopted textbooks.
Wonder and excitement about reading.	Check with all subject area teachers and librarians about student reading habits.	Develop strategies for exciting students and teachers about the value of reading.

Also, the tasks of program evaluation will become much more manageable, particularly in the long run, if they are well organized. A major step in this organization is the establishment of a regular data collection system so that what is learned from the various parts of the total program evaluation flows smoothly among them. Many tests are given to students in nearly all schools, and, taken collectively, they furnish a wealth of information about them. In most schools, however, this rich information is, at best, very inefficiently used. Tests, observations, and summary analyses should be scheduled so that the results they yield come at the appropriate times to enable decisions about the school program and about other elements of the evaluation plan. We will demonstrate how this scheduling may be accomplished in an elementary school, a middle school, and a high school.

TYPES OF TESTS USED BY SCHOOLS

Before we explore this scheduling, let us consider the variety of different types of tests that are typically given in the school. Although there is some overlap among them, we identify and briefly define seven different types of assessment tools that are regularly used in schools: aptitude tests, diagnostic tests, minimum competency tests, readiness tests, standardized achievement tests, student portfolios, and teacher-made tests. These brief definitions and the discussion that follows are abstracted from the work of Worthen, Borg, and White (1993). We recommend that the principal examine this source carefully for additional guidance in selecting and using tests.

- *Aptitude Tests*: Tests of student ability necessary for or supportive of student performance in some set of activities.

- *Diagnostic Tests*: In-depth tests of achievement designed to assess student ability to perform specific skills within a complex task.

- *Minimum Competency Tests*: Criterion-referenced objective tests mandated by the government.

- *Readiness Tests*: Tests of student attainment of the skills, knowledge, attitudes, and other behavioral traits needed to efficiently engage in some aspect of school instruction.

♦ *Standardized Achievement Tests*: Tests of student mastery of academic knowledge and skill under standard conditions of test instructions, time limits, and materials used in administering and scoring.

♦ *Student Portfolios*: Progressive samples of student work used to document student accomplishments in various areas of the curriculum.

♦ *Teacher-made Tests*: Measures of academic knowledge and skill created by teachers.

The challenge for the principal is to coordinate these tests so that useful decisions can be made regarding the educational program. The clues to how they fit together can be inferred from the definitions above. For example, as we examine the scores on the state's minimum competency test, a number of key questions come to mind. The first and most obvious question is: *How well did the school do overall?* But we should realize that while this is an important question, it is also a fairly shallow one. Two other questions should immediately come to mind: *Who did well on the test and who didn't?* and *What in the test did they do well on and what didn't they do so well on?* This means that we will need to disaggregate our test results to see which individual students and identifiable groups of students failed to attain the minimum competency level and in what areas of academic attainment they fell short. This, in turn, will lead to an examination of our curriculum to see if in fact we have taught the required knowledge and skills and to reconsider how we teach them. It can also lead to further diagnostic testing for particular students to identify the specific subtasks that must be mastered before more holistic mastery can be achieved.

Standardized achievement tests can provide a similar service. In their case, however, they show us not how well our students did in regard to a state-mandated criterion, but how they compare with other students across the nation in regard to identified areas of academic attainment. Results may lead to inspection and adjustment of the curriculum or to further diagnostic testing. However, if our review of the test results shows us that the test is measuring something we are not trying to teach and have no intention of trying to teach (at least not at the grade levels being assessed by the test), we may decide to use a different standardized achievement test. If what the test measures is not what we're teaching, we should either change the test or change what we're teaching. Any other decision (or indecision) results in a waste of resources.

Similar statements can be made about teacher assessments, whether teacher-made tests of academic achievement or alternative measures such as student portfolios. Do they measure how well students are doing with reference to the goals we have for them (whether in terms of broader student outcomes or in regard to the more narrow objectives of a particular unit)? If students have mastered certain objectives, what do they need to learn next? If they have failed to master the objectives, what type of re-teaching or additional learning is required?

Readiness tests and aptitude tests can add considerably to the efficiency of the teaching/learning process if properly used. Readiness tests help us to know when students are developmentally ready for certain types of learning, such as reading or mathematics. They can also suggest tasks and experiences that will support needed development. Aptitude tests can help us take advantage of particular student potential and, accordingly, help us shape educational experiences to maximize the development of that potential.

SCHOOL TESTING SCHEDULES

To show how the various types of tests that are typically used in schools may be scheduled so that the results flow efficiently, we have included possible testing schedules for an elementary school (Figure 4.3), a middle school (Figure 4.4), and a high school (Figure 4.5).

As we examine the testing plan presented in Figure 4.3, we can see how different types of tests can be related to each other in a systematic fashion. In the first two columns, we see the measures that might be used by a typical elementary school in its pre-kindergarten and kindergarten programs: readiness tests, diagnostic tests, and student portfolios. By using readiness tests and diagnostic tests the school seeks to get a picture of how

FIGURE 4.3. POSSIBLE STUDENT TESTING PLAN FOR AN ELEMENTARY SCHOOL (PRE-K–5)

		Pre-K	K	1	2	3	4	5
A	Standardized Achievement Tests				X (General Achievement Test)			X (General Achievement Test)
B	Readiness Tests	X	X					
C	Aptitude Tests				X (General Intelligence Test)	X (GT Identification)	X (GT Identification)	X (GT Identification)
D	Diagnostic Tests (as needed)	X	X	X	X	X	X	X
E	Teacher-Made Tests			X	X	X	X	X
F	Student Portfolios	X	X	X	X	X	X	X
G	Minimum Competency Tests					X (Reading, Mathematics)	X (Reading, Mathematics, Writing)	X (Reading, Mathematics)

FIGURE 4.4. POSSIBLE STUDENT TESTING PLAN FOR A MIDDLE SCHOOL (6–8)

		6	7	8
A	Standardized Achievement Tests			X (General Achievement Test)
B	Readiness Tests	X (Algebra Readiness Test)		
C	Aptitude Tests	X (GT Identification)	X (GT Identification)	X (GT Identification)
D	Diagnostic Tests (as needed)	X	X	X
E	Teacher-Made Tests	X	X	X
F	Student Portfolios	X	X	X
G	Minimum Competency Tests	X (Reading, Mathematics)	X (Reading, Mathematics)	X (Reading, Writing, Mathematics Science, Social Studies)

FIGURE 4.5. POSSIBLE STUDENT TESTING PLAN FOR A HIGH SCHOOL (9–12)

		9	10	11	12
A	Standardized Achievement Tests		X (Advanced Placement)	X (General Achievement Advanced Placement)	X (Advanced Placement)
B	Readiness Tests				
C	Aptitude Tests	X (DAT)	X (PSAT)	X (SAT/ACT)	X (SAT/ACT)
D	Diagnostic Tests (as needed)	X	X	X	X
E	Teacher-Made Tests	X	X	X	X
F	Student Portfolios	X	X	X	X
G	Minimum Competency Tests		X (Reading, Writing, Mathematics)	X (Retest as needed)	X (Retest as needed)

students are likely to respond to the academic program ahead of them and, through this information, to shape its overall instructional program and the individual programs of students. Student portfolios demonstrate the early school accomplishments of these young students.

As we proceed across the grades represented by the successive columns, we can see how the school builds on this early information. In the first grade, teacher-made tests that assess particular classroom objectives are added to student portfolios to evaluate progress of individual students and to shape subsequent classroom offerings. Readiness tests are no longer typically used, although diagnostic tests to assess individual learning needs are continued in order to enable the school to make necessary adjustments. Beginning in the second grade, the school begins to identify students with special aptitude so that they can receive special instruction to capitalize on their ability.

In the second grade, a standardized achievement test is given to see how well the students are performing academically in comparison to other students across the nation. Three years later, in fifth grade, the students again take a standardized achievement test to see if their comparative academic status has improved, deteriorated, or remained the same.

A state-mandated test is given for the first time in the third grade to determine whether students are attaining basic competency in key academic skill areas. This test looks at their skill attainment in the areas of reading and mathematics in third grade, and then adds writing skills to the list in the fourth grade.

Again, we remind the reader that there are both individual and programmatic considerations in this testing plan. At the individual level we are seeking information that will enable us to shape the school's instructional program to best meet the needs and potential of each student. At the programmatic level, we are seeking information that will show us how to structure the instructional program so that it will systematically meet these individual instructional needs. For the individual we are asking, *What must be done to meet this student's instructional needs?* With regard to the instructional program we are asking, *How can we allocate resources and structure procedures to meet student needs in the most effective and efficient manner?* As we noted in Chapter 2, the principal needs to move easily between these two levels.

What we have described about the student testing plan for the elementary school (Figure 4.3, p. 67) applies generally to the student testing plans for the middle school (Figure 4.4, p. 68) and high school (Figure 4.5, p. 69). The only major difference occurs at the high school level, where different types of aptitude tests appear. At ninth grade the Differential Aptitude Tests (DAT) are used to determine student aptitudes for different vocations for the purpose of providing specific direction for the remainder of their school programs. In grades 10, 11, and 12, the Scholastic Aptitude Test (SAT) is given to assess students' aptitude for success in college.

While these schedules have been abstracted from the actual testing schedules of a number of different schools, please keep in mind that they are intended to be merely illustrative. The testing schedule of a particular school must be shaped to fit its own needs. We hope, however, that we have challenged you to consider the testing schedule in any school or school district in light of two related questions:

- ◆ Can the testing schedule efficiently facilitate educational decisions at the school, the school district and individual classroom levels?
- ◆ Are the tests in use in a school or school district actually being used in an efficient and effective way to make decisions?

As the reader examines these testing schedules, he or she should ask essentially the same evaluation questions that we have been asking since the beginning of this chapter: *What is being evaluated? How is it being evaluated? What will be done with the results of the evaluation?*

BROADENING THE SCOPE OF PROGRAM EVALUATION

What we have said about program evaluation thus far applies to program evaluation at various levels: at a classroom level, at a school level, or at a school district level. It also applies to a particular program (e.g., the reading program that we examined), to a funded project (e.g., a state grant designed to promote classroom usage of technology), or to some part of the educational program that is not directly associated with student academic attainment (e.g., the school discipline plan or the athletic program). In each case, it is useful to remember our three basic questions: *What should be evaluated? (Why should it be evaluated?), How should it be evaluated?* and *What will be done with the results of the evaluation?*

Thus far our evaluation has been confined to the type of data and analysis that would be collected for an objectives-oriented evaluation. While this type of evaluation has a long history, it also has certain shortcomings, which we have noted. In particular, we have not paid much attention to the context in which student achievement is occurring. We will take some time now to pay attention to that and to consider the implications of another program evaluation approach.

APPLYING THE CIPP MODEL

Let us consider what the implications would be if we used a management-oriented approach, such as the CIPP model (Figure 4.1, p. 52). We would need to consider, first of all, the C, *context evaluation*. This focuses our attention on the goals of the evaluation and returns us to our first basic question: *what should be evaluated* and its corollary, *why should it be evaluated?* Thus far, we have not made a major shift in our evaluation procedures.

But consider the second element of the CIPP model: *input evaluation*. Here we are making decisions that will structure how personnel, procedures, materials, facilities, time, and budget should be allocated to the program that we are evaluating. How do we determine how much time should be allocated to instruction in the various phases of the educational program? What are the staffing needs of the program? What curriculum materials and other materials should be used in the program? Clearly the success of the program is dependent to some degree upon the quality and combination of resources that support it, and any future decisions about the program will require sufficient information about the nature and impact of these resources so that data-based decisions can be made about their acquisition and allocation.

The third element of the CIPP model, *process evaluation*, focuses our attention on the processes by which the program is implemented. It is commonly recognized that for every school that implements a particular program (e.g., a science or reading program) there will be a somewhat different application depending upon the context of the particular school. Years ago, James Gallagher (1967) found that even for a very highly structured science program there was, in effect, a different curriculum, taught by each teacher who implemented it. Educational programs as envisioned by the school district, or even by the building leadership, are never exactly the same as what actually happens in a particular classroom. Clearly, then, if we are to evaluate the impact of the various facets of an educational program, we must have a clear picture of the processes that were used to implement them. If, in our *input evaluation*, we were concerned with the personal and professional characteristics of the teachers assigned to the program, here, in *process evaluation*, we are concerned with what the teachers actually do. Much of our personnel evaluation strategies will be devoted to understanding what teachers do and to helping them shape their efforts to better support the instructional goals of the school.

Finally, of course, we must look at *product evaluation*, the attainments and outcomes of the program, not only at the end of a program cycle, but as often as necessary during the course of the cycle. However, our third basic question (*What will be done with the results of the evaluation?*) reminds us that even after we examine the outcomes (through tests, observations, portfolios, or whatever) it is not enough simply to record the results. The outcomes must serve our ongoing decisions about: what modifications we need to make in the educational program to make it better serve our educational goals; what modifications we need to make in the educational program to make it better serve the needs of particular students; and what modifications we need to make in the goals themselves. These modified goals, richer and better directed from what we have learned through program evaluation, give direction to the next cycle of our program evaluation.

OTHER APPROACHES

We will not take the space here to do so, but principals will find it profitable to consider how each of the other program evaluation approaches could strengthen the school's efforts. For example, the *naturalistic and participant-oriented approaches* could serve the principal by reviewing the evaluation from many sides to see that critical elements are not being excluded from the evaluation and that the interests of all the school's legitimate stakeholders are being served. In a similar manner, *expertise-oriented evaluations* can often be useful in obtaining the insights of people with particular areas of expertise to lend their assistance to the school's evaluation. *Consumer-oriented evaluations* may help principals in making decisions for their schools as consumers of educational products, and enable them to consider the legitimate needs of those who, in effect, purchase their products: taxpayers, parents, and students. As we noted earlier, an *adversary-oriented approach,* if used judiciously, can help the principal avoid many of the dangers of bias in evaluation and can enrich the evaluation.

INTEGRATING A FACULTY EVALUATION PLAN

We can evaluate many aspects of the school's operation and, as we have seen, we can evaluate them in a variety of ways. If, however, information from these separate evaluations is not integrated with a comprehensive plan to serve overall goals, they will, at the very best, be inefficient, and they might, at the very worst, be counterproductive and disruptive to the operation of the school. We will take some time in this section to illustrate how one type of evaluation, faculty evaluation, that is common to nearly all schools can be structured and integrated to serve the overall goals of the educational program.

Faculty evaluation can be considered at two different levels. Like instructional evaluation, faculty evaluation may be considered at both an individual level and a programmatic level. We are concerned about the instructional effectiveness and professional growth of each teacher in the school; but we are also concerned about how well our development and allocation of these valuable human resources serves our overall programmatic goals. Obviously, the two levels of faculty evaluation must be synchronous: our evaluation of individual teachers must provide information that is directed to programmatic questions.

As noted earlier, faculty evaluation is related to both *input evaluation* and *process evaluation*. Teachers are a basic resource that must be obtained in advance of program implementation and allocated to the program in a manner that effectively serves the educational program. We can evaluate this resource allocation as part of our input evaluation. Teachers are usually the chief implementers of an educational program. How they implement is a concern of process evaluation.

At the same time, teacher evaluation, as a component of the total program evaluation, is a cyclical process that may itself be described by the CIPP model. This cyclical process is shown in Figure 4.6. The process begins with the *mission of the school* that informs *recruitment and selection* of teachers, *establishes initial professional development plans* for teachers, and then follows teachers through subsequent *formative evaluation, summative evaluation,* and the *renewal of their professional development plans.* At every stage of the cycle, both programmatic and individual dimensions must be considered.

RECRUITMENT AND SELECTION

Every school should maintain a clear, comprehensive picture of what it expects its faculty as a whole to contribute to the attainment of the goals of the school. Part of this picture is an awareness of its current faculty strengths and needs. Expectations for an individual teacher's contributions to the school (*context evaluation*) are derived from this overall picture and are set at the time a teacher is recruited and hired. Recall here our brief discussion of merit and worth in Chapter 2. A prospective teacher may have great merit and may have been an exemplary teacher at a previous school. However, our chief concern is with the worth of this teacher to our school in terms of how well his or her expertise serves our school goals in conjunction with the efforts of other teachers and the configuration of instructional strategies at our school. Consider how crucial it is that expectations for each teacher be clear and be dynamically supportive of the educational program. The principal who is willing to settle

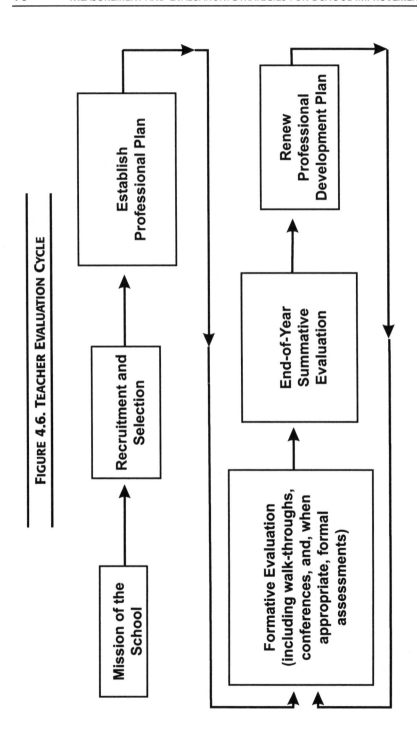

FIGURE 4.6. TEACHER EVALUATION CYCLE

Mission of the School

Recruitment and Selection

Establish Professional Plan

Formative Evaluation (including walk-throughs, conferences, and, when appropriate, formal assessments)

End-of-Year Summative Evaluation

Renew Professional Development Plan

for nearly any teacher who has a reasonably accommodating personality and the necessary state certification is likely to get exactly that and no more. Each new teacher should strengthen the total instructional team (teachers, administrators, counselors, etc.) that is the core of the educational program, and the strategies for integrating that teacher into the team should be clearly specified. Obviously, a principal will be wise to use the team in the recruitment and hiring process.

INITIAL PROFESSIONAL DEVELOPMENT PLAN

Plans for the professional development of each teacher should begin immediately and should flow directly from the hiring decision. Specific goals designed to strengthen each teacher's contribution to the educational program should be set collaboratively with the teacher (*context evaluation*), and resources, in terms of time, guidelines, materials, staff development, and other support, should be allocated (*input evaluation*) to make it possible for the teacher to reach those goals.

FORMATIVE EVALUATION

The teacher's performance in the classroom and interaction with students, parents, and other teachers should be monitored through walk-throughs, conferences, and, when necessary, formal assessments. The purpose of this formative evaluation is to provide feedback on what is happening (*process evaluation*) so that the teacher can modify, eliminate, or extend what he or she does in order to increase educational efficiency and effectiveness. Principals, using their own professional expertise and that of their entire faculties, can play important roles in strengthening the performance of every teacher in their schools.

SUMMATIVE EVALUATION AND RENEWAL OF THE PROFESSIONAL DEVELOPMENT PLAN

At the end of the year, it is the responsibility of the principal to ensure that a careful summative evaluation is provided to each teacher. These separate summative evaluations are aggregated to provide important information to the principal and faculty as they determine overall faculty strengths and weaknesses. This information about faculty strengths and weaknesses is combined with new challenges the school is facing to identify the new staffing and training needs that must be met to support the educational program.

Often, summative evaluation is linked specifically to making decisions about firing, hiring, promotions, or new assignments. However, it should be considered much more broadly than this. This is the time to determine if (and to what extent) the goals envisioned for teacher, students, and indeed the entire educational program, that were stated in the professional development plan have been achieved (*product evaluation*). This is also the time to determine, in a summative manner, what prevented certain goals from being reached. Was it a matter of time? Were inappropriate teaching methods the cause? Were teaching materials inappropriate? Were the goals unrealistic goals? Answers to these questions lead to new professional development plans for teachers (*context evaluation*) that include new goals and new allocations of resources.

Thus, the cycle continues on an annual basis. Careful evaluation following this cycle paves the way for systematic measurable improvement in teaching and obviously is in the best interests of teachers, students, and all the other school stakeholders. Sloppy evaluation leads to misunderstanding, misappropriation of resources, and frustration on the part of all stakeholders.

In Chapter 2, we examined the Program Evaluation Standards published by the Joint Committee on Standards for Educational Evaluation (1994). In 1988, the Joint Committee published the Personnel Evaluation Standards. This latter set of standards is divided into the same four categories of standards (propriety standards, utility standards, feasibility standards, and accuracy standards) that were applied to the Program Evaluation Standards and are generally parallel to them. They provide a valuable complementary resource to the Program Evaluation Standards in designing and implementing a comprehensive program evaluation in the school.

SOME FINAL THOUGHTS ABOUT PROGRAM EVALUATION

Program evaluation is the chief strategy available to the principal and faculty as they determine a direction for the school, plan procedures to support that direction, monitor implementation of those procedures, and assess the attainment of the goals that they have established. In their book on *Problem Analysis*, a volume in the *School Leadership Library*, Achilles, Reynolds, and Achilles (1997) distinguish between problem-finding and problem-solving. Program evaluation is addressed to both. Program evaluation, properly considered, involves both framing the questions that the school ought to address and generating information that yields useful answers and better questions.

Program evaluation in a school is a complex process, incorporating the many programs that operate in it and also the information that is derived from the evaluation of individuals as they operate in those programs. A program, according to the Joint Committee on Standards for Educational Evaluation, is made up of "educational activities that are provided on a continuing basis" (1994, p. 3). Thus, a reading program, a discipline program, and an athletic program are all proper subjects for program evaluation. These separate program evaluations must be coordinated by an overall program evaluation design.

There is a danger that, as we attempt to organize and systematize our evaluation efforts, we will fail to maintain sufficient flexibility to allow for evaluation of new projects (e.g., an individually paced algebra program, a mentoring program for students with special needs, etc.). The principal who would be responsive to the changing context in which the school operates must take a stance that allows for response to new evaluation requirements as they arise. For any new project or program in the school, the principal needs to ask the same questions that would be asked about the traditional elements of the school program: *What should be evaluated, how should it be evaluated, and what will be done with the results of the evaluation?* The principal also must take care to ensure that these new evaluation efforts are integrated with the school's overall evaluation efforts and the cycles in which they are administered. It is possible for an evaluation plan to become so complex that it begins to have a negative impact on the programs it is attempting to evaluate.

Finally, the principal must never forget that the purpose of program evaluation is improvement of the educational program of the school. This means that evaluation must be linked directly to significant educational goals. At the same time, the principal must realize that significant progress is made systematically and realistically. Clear benchmarks for growth in every aspect of the school's operation (reading scores, faculty development, etc.) must be set, and progress toward them must be monitored. The evaluation that comes from this monitoring must show clear direction for plotting growth and setting future benchmarks. Effective administration of a comprehensive, integrated program evaluation is one of the most powerful leadership strategies that the principal can implement.

ACTION FOLLOW-UP

1. Identify a significant program in your school that should be evaluated. This can either be an instructional program (e.g., the mathematics program), an instructional support program (e.g., a discipline program), or a new program or special project (e.g., a remedial reading program or a computer-assisted instruction (CAI) project). Develop a basic evaluation plan for this program (as demonstrated in Figure 4.2, p. 63) that responds to the three basic questions: *What should be evaluated? How should it be evaluated? What will be done with the results of the evaluation?*

2. Apply the CIPP Model to the program you have chosen to evaluate.

   a. As a first step in this application, make a list of questions that you would like to address to each of the four types of evaluation: *context, input, process, and product.*

b. Describe briefly how these questions have been answered in the past and how you will continue to seek information to answer these questions.

c. Develop a plan for obtaining more complete answers to these questions.

d. Develop a diagram that shows how the *context, input, process and product evaluations* relate to each other to serve the overall purposes of program evaluation.

PART II

MEASUREMENT

5

WHAT EVERY PRINCIPAL SHOULD KNOW ABOUT MEASUREMENT

This chapter deals with measurement. It is designed to provide principals with an overview of basic measurement concepts, issues, and strategies that have direct application on the job. This is accomplished by using a self-appraisal system. The system is constructed in a question and answer format. There are 30 questions. The questions are organized into seven general sections. Each section reflects a primary area of basic measurement concerns.

With this in mind, readers are encouraged to use this self-appraisal system as follows. First, read each question. Next, formulate a response to the question. Finally, compare your response to the answer given in the book. For best results, we suggest that all questions in the self-appraisal system be addressed in the order given in the text. If readers plan to complete their self-appraisals in more than one session, individual sections provide logical break points.

The answer provided in the text for each question includes a direct reference to one or more basic sources the reader can explore for more detailed information. Thus, the appraisal system also provides a self-study guide principals can use to extend their knowledge and develop new skills.

Three decision rules guided the selection of basic sources. First, the actual number of sources referenced was held to a minimum. We believe this decision rule will help principals to better focus individual self-study plans. Second, the initial selection of specific sources was based on our experience in conducting measurement and evaluation courses and continuing education exercises for school principals. We believe this decision rule reflects our preference for beginning self-study with more practical rather than theoretical treatments of basic measurement concerns. Third, the final selection of specific sources was based on the need for each selected source to identify other references that provide principals additional practical guidelines for learning to determine the quality and utility of an educational measure; constructing and using new measures, such as teacher-made tests and needs assessment questionnaires; and finding, selecting, and using existing measures, such as standardized achievement tests and published school climate instruments.

Some principals may already be familiar with a basic measurement text which is not included in this chapter. Others might be currently enrolled in a graduate measurement and evaluation course that uses a basic text not referenced here. If one or both of these situations is relevant, we recommend that you integrate these familiar sources into your self-study strategy.

MEASUREMENT CONCEPTS

Although measurement is a familiar activity in the schools, its function and utility are not always well understood. Our purpose in the first section is to explore your understanding of educational measurement and to create a framework for more specific ideas that follow in other sections of the appraisal system.

Question 1. What is measurement?

A desktop reference for defining many common terms encountered in educational measurement and evaluation is the *Evaluation Thesaurus* authored by Michael Scriven (1991). In this thesaurus, Scriven suggests that measurement is the determination of the magnitude of a quantity. In more general terms, he argues that measurement is a process.

This process typically yields measurements that are expressed in one of three forms: *continuous scores* (such as integers used to reflect IQ scores); *ranks* (such as letter grades, percentiles, or rank orders that classify entities of interest as first, second, third, and so forth); and *categories* (such as yes or no responses to a question, or a classification system that allows one to describe school districts as urban, suburban, or rural). Scriven calls the three corresponding processes *numerical scoring, ranking,* and *labeling.*

In psychological testing and other behavior research strategies, measurement is typically defined only in quantitative terms. For example, Leary (1995) suggests that "the goal of measurement is to assign numbers to objects or events (such as behaviors) in such a way that the numbers correspond in some meaningful way to the attribute we are trying to measure" (p. 56).

From the perspective of variability, Leary argues that behavioral science researchers want the variability in the numbers assigned to reflect, as precisely as possible, the variability in the attribute being measured. A perfect measure would be one for which the variability in the numbers provided by the measure corresponded perfectly with the actual (true) variability in the object or event measured. Departures from this perfect correspondence are called measurement errors. Accordingly, an excellent measurement instrument is one that has very small measurement errors.

Question 2. What are the four most widely used measures in educational research and evaluation projects?

There are many types of procedures for measuring human characteristics and behaviors in educational organizations. In a book aimed at making research strategies as accessible as possible to educational practitioners, Borg, Gall, and Gall (1993) note the most common measurement procedures for collecting data to be used in program evaluation and action research in the schools are the following:

 ◆ Paper-and-pencil tests
 ◆ Questionnaires
 ◆ Interviews

♦ Direct Observations

Each of these four data collection strategies is the basis for a series of questions to be addressed later in this self-appraisal system.

At this point it is helpful to recognize that both paper-and-pencil tests and questionnaires are similar in that they typically use predetermined (quantitative) scales to measure variables of interest. Moreover, both of these measurement procedures rely on self-reports.

Interviews, on the other hand, involve the collection of qualitative information through direct interaction between the interviewer and the individuals being studied.

Direct observation involves the use of observers to count and record the frequency of specific, clearly defined behaviors. For example, principals often use direct observation instruments to measure and evaluate teaching in classrooms. Included in these measurement instruments are specific teaching behavior categories (or tasks), such as using *advanced* organizers and *student motivators* to introduce a lesson.

Question 3. Behavioral science researchers frequently make a distinction between measurement and archival data. What is implied in this distinction?

Leary (1995) notes that in most inquiries, measurement is *contemporaneous*. It occurs at the time a new research or evaluation project is conducted. Accordingly, the investigator designs a study, recruits participants, and then collects data about those participants using a predesigned behavioral measure, such as a test, questionnaire, interview protocol, or a direct observation guide.

On the other hand, some research and evaluation projects are conducted using data that were collected *prior to the time* a new inquiry is undertaken. Accordingly, the investigator in this type of inquiry (often called archival research) analyzes data pulled from existing data sources, such as test score reports, school records, personal correspondences, memoranda, student report cards, and so on. In most instances, these archival data were collected for purposes other than the specific intent guiding a new inquiry.

As you learned in earlier chapters, both new measures and archival data can be (and almost always are) used in a single program evaluation. Using this distinction, principals who wish to conduct efficient and timely program evaluation projects often begin these inquiries by first clearly defining the purpose of their inquiry and then asking two specific questions. First, what archival data can be used in the project? Second, what measures must be designed (or selected) to collect relevant data not already available on the campus or in the school district?

> **Question 4. The domain of interest in this text is *measurement and evaluation*. While it is heuristic to combine these two terms to describe a single domain, there is a clear distinction between measurement and evaluation. What is this distinction?**

In the response to question 1, we learned that measurement is the process of making empirical observations of some attribute or characteristic and translating these observations into numerical or categorical form using clearly defined procedures and rules.

In the *Evaluation Thesaurus*, Scriven (1991) notes that evaluation is "the process of determining the merit, worth and value of things, and evaluations are the products of that process" (p. 1). In the thesaurus, *merit* is described as the intrinsic value of a program, person, or activity and *worth* is the value of that program, person, or activity in relationship to a specific purpose. Thus, merit deals with *intrinsic value* (a value decision based on its own specific intent) and worth deals with *external value* (a value decision based on an external criterion).

These descriptions acknowledge that both measurement and evaluation are processes. However, measurement is the process used to collect data on which evaluative judgments are made. Measurement is *not* in and of itself an evaluation activity.

> **Question 5. In practice and professional study we often encounter the combined term *educational tests and measurements*. While these**

terms represent a single domain of interest to educators, there is a basic distinction between tests and measurements. What is this distinction?

Following the logic in Worthen, Borg, and White (1993), *educational measurement* is broader than *educational testing*. While measurement frequently uses tests, it can also employ direct observation instruments, use of checklists and other data collection methods that cannot precisely be classified as tests. In a word, testing is only one form of measurement.

USES OF EDUCATIONAL MEASURES

The second section of the self-appraisal system centers on the use of educational measures in program evaluation and decision making. Two basic references guided the development and organization of questions used here.

The scope and sequence of questions draws heavily from the comprehensive treatment of measurement and evaluation in the schools given in Worthen, Borg, and White (1993). This source is especially noteworthy for its up-to-date treatment of both the ethical and legal concerns that should guide principals and their professional colleagues in using educational measures to improve teaching and learning.

The second influential source is Scriven (1991), who argues that testing is the most common procedure for determining the success of students and for reaching decisions regarding the effectiveness of particular teaching methods or curricula. This perspective led us to use testing as the primary domain of interest.

Following Scriven's (1991) recommendation, we think of tests in this section as simply the name for any specific and explicit effort to determine the performance or attitudes of students and teachers. This strategy should make the information provided in this section relevant for understanding the value of a wide array of educational measures used in the schools.

Question 6. When properly designed and appropriately applied by qualified professionals, tests yield results that can be used by a wide

range of people. In general terms, who are some of the stakeholder groups (interested parties) likely to use test results?

Worthen, Borg, and White (1993) suggest that in education, virtually everyone is a test user. They identified these ten stakeholder groups:

- Teachers
- Students
- Parents
- Principals
- School psychologists
- School counselors
- Lawmakers and policymakers
- Research and evaluation directors
- News reporters
- Lawyers

Question 7. How might each stakeholder group identified in the previous question use test results?

Many possible uses of test results can be linked to each stakeholder group. Moreover, some stakeholders can qualify for membership in more than one group. For example, teachers and counselors may also be parents, principals may also be students in graduate school, and so forth. For comparative purposes, here is an overview of the responses given in Worthen, Borg, and White (1993):

> *Teachers* use test results to determine students' progress in learning specific knowledge or skills.
>
> *Students* use test results to discover if they are learning what they are expected to learn.
>
> *Parents* use test results to determine how well their children are doing in school.
>
> *Principals* use test results to determine how well students in their schools are learning.

School psychologists use test results to assess a student's strengths and special needs.

School counselors use test results to guide students in selecting courses of study and careers.

Lawmakers and policy makers use test results to establish educational priorities and to allocate resources.

Researchers and evaluation directors use test results to assess the effectiveness of particular school programs, teaching strategies and support services.

News reporters use test results to report on the quality of schooling and other educational policy issues.

Lawyers use test results to determine the legality of particular educational processes.

Question 8. While there is clearly a wide range of reasons why stakeholders use test results, educational researchers have suggested that these reasons can be placed into a few general categories based on the types of decisions that are made using test results. What are these basic types of decisions?

A content analysis of several educational test and measurement sources led Worthen, Borg, and White (1993) to specify five types of decisions that are likely to be based on test results. These are summarized below.

- ◆ **Direct Instructional Decisions** are decisions made by teachers and principals about ongoing activities in the classroom. Included are immediate instructional decisions (decisions to be made on the spot and that often depend on informal assessment), grading decisions, diagnostic decisions (decisions about the learning progress of a student or a class) and instructional planning decisions.

- ◆ **Instructional Management Decisions** are decisions dealing with the placement of students in situations where they are most likely to succeed. These decisions are typically made by principals, psychologists, counselors, or committees. Such decisions deal either with *classification and placement* (for example, using test results to sort ninth grade students into remedial, standard, or honors mathematics) or with *counseling and guidance* (for example, helping students in their career planning and personal adjustments).

♦ **Entry-Exit Decisions** are decisions dealing with who should enter particular institutions or programs of study (selection decisions) and who has completed the requirements for a program of study (certification decisions). For this category Worthen, Borg, and White (1993) remind us that there is a distinction between *placement* and *selection* decisions. In placement, everyone gets placed. In selection, there is a limitation on who participates. Specifically, some candidates will be selected and others will be rejected.

♦ **Program, Administrative and Policy Decisions** are decisions that affect educational programs, curricula, or total organizations. Included are program decisions (Which of two algebra I programs is more effective?), administrative decisions (What are the specific objectives we need to address in our new strategic plan?), and policy decisions (What priorities should guide the allocation of funds to individual schools?).

♦ **Research Decisions** are decisions associated with expanding our knowledge base. Such decisions center on finding effective and efficient means to expand our current knowledge base about educational processes.

In the *Encyclopedia of Educational Research,* Linn (1992) provides an alternate response using eight rather than five general categories to represent the types of decisions to be made using test results. His categories are:

- Assessment of Achieved Competence
- Diagnosis of Strengths and Weaknesses
- Assignment of Grades
- Certification and Promotion
- Advanced Placement and Credit by Examination
- Curriculum and Program Evaluation
- Accountability
- Informing Educational Policy

Both responses support the position that tests and other assessment instruments *can* provide relevant information for effective educational decision making. We emphasize *can* so that readers will keep this idea in mind: Tests and other assessment instruments are relevant only to the extent that these educational measures are well designed (valid and reliable) and correctly used by competent (qualified) decision makers. This concern is revisited in subsequent sections of the self-appraisal system.

Question 9. What are some of the recent developments and trends in educational measurement that provide the current context for measurement and evaluation in the schools?

Over the past three decades, increasing public demand for educational accountability has caused professional educators and policymakers to rethink their responsibilities for specifying educational outcomes and for providing more accurate ways to document them.

Worthen, Borg, and White (1993, Chapter 2) have suggested that these persistent public demands for higher levels of accountability (beginning in the mid-1960s) can be linked directly to the important trends and development in educational measurement. Moreover, they believe that these ten trends, which began with the design of the National Assessment of Educational Progress in 1964, provide the current context for measurement and evaluation in the schools. In chronological order, their ten trends are:

1. National Assessment of Educational Progress (an annual national assessment in ten subject areas);

2. The Accountability Movement (legislative mandates that required school districts to report test results to state officials and lawmakers);

3. The Trend Toward Criterion-Referenced Measurement (the shift away from norm-referenced tests and toward criterion-referenced tests);

4. Trends in Scholastic Aptitude and Achievement Test Scores (a reaction to the significant annual downward trends in standardized test results between the mid-1960s and the early 1980s);

5. The Establishment of Minimum Competence Testing Programs (primarily a political strategy mandating the use of criterion-referenced, objective tests to counter continued lack of confidence in American schools);

6. Renewed Calls for Reform in Educational Measurement (criticisms of standardized tests that led to a growing body of literature on the effects of using standardized tests to make high-stakes decisions);

7. Development of Professional Organizations for Measurement Specialists (improvement efforts that produced standards for educational and psychological testing);

8. Positions Taken by Professional Associations toward Measurement Issues (a movement yielding published professional support and opposition to testing practices in the schools);

9. The Use of Competency Tests for Teacher Certification (another mandated effort aimed at making American schools more accountable);

10. Calls for Alternative Performance Measures (also called *authentic* assessment of student performance, these reform efforts were designed to counter the practice of using traditional standardized tests as the sole indicator of quality schools).

A comprehensive treatment of these national trends is beyond the scope of this chapter. Accordingly, we focus here on just one trend. Specifically, the next two questions on minimum competency testing (trend 5) are used to illustrate how these national trends directly influence current practice at the school level.

For those who wish to explore the historical roots that have shaped today's use of educational measurement, we recommend Worthen, Borg, and White (1993) and the *Encyclopedia of Educational Research* (Alkin, 1992). Some specific encyclopedia terms we found helpful to start this exploration are achievement testing; competency testing; performance measurement; standards for tests and ethical test use; and test construction.

Question 10. What is minimum competency testing?

The certification of minimum skills is a practice used in settings as diverse as issuing a driver's license, authorizing a physician to practice medicine, or certifying teachers to work in the schools. Thinking in terms of students, minimum competency testing refers to using tests to certify that students are able to demonstrate their mastery of certain minimal skills. In many instances, minimum competency testing is referenced as just *competency testing*.

Jaeger (1992) has identified several current uses of competency tests in the schools. He notes that the most frequent use is to provide a standard for awarding a high school diploma. In some states and individual school districts, students must earn passing scores on formal competency tests in order to be promoted. This use of competency tests is typically restricted to a few grades that mark transitions between designated levels of education (such as elementary to middle school or middle school to high school).

In addition, Jaeger (1992) notes that competency tests are also used to permit students to graduate from high school prior to the completion of 12th grade and to qualify high school students for college credit. Historically speaking, Oosterhof (1990) argues that "the minimum competency testing movement is largely a response to concerns about an overall drop in academic achievement and a view that high school diplomas were increasingly becoming a certificate of attendance rather than academic achievement" (p. 395).

As a consequence, almost all states now require students to be tested for competence. Moreover, in a majority of states, students are now legally obligated to demonstrate *minimum competency* results to receive a high school diploma.

Question 11. What are the characteristics of minimum competency testing that will withstand legal challenges?

Minimum competency testing requirements that impose sanctions on students failing to pass the test will no doubt continue to be challenged in the immediate future. Moreover, recent court cases have defined the characteristics of minimum competency that will withstand legal challenges.

Using the research findings offered by Madus (1983) on lawsuits filed between 1974 and 1983, Worthen, Borg, and White (1993, Chapter 3) provide this list of characteristics that will withstand legal challenges:

- ♦ Valid objectives describing skills that are truly basic competencies.
- ♦ A test that is a valid measure of those objectives.
- ♦ Evidence that the skills assessed are actually reflected in the curriculum and taught in the classroom.
- ♦ Early assessment and identification of those needing remedial help.
- ♦ Provision of remedial help for all who require it.
- ♦ Sufficient advance notice and multiple opportunities to pass the competency test.

Because the many issues surrounding minimum competency testing are not likely to be fully resolved soon, Worthen and his colleagues offer this recommendation: "Any educational agency contemplating the use of minimum competency testing would be well advised to assure that their program meets the six criteria implicit in Madus's list" (p. 43). Clearly, these criteria should also be kept in mind by principals currently developing or revising competency tests in their schools.

> **Question 12. A key legal issue in the use of tests and other educational measures in the schools is the right to privacy. What guidelines should principals establish in their schools to ensure that privacy rights and confidentiality are protected?**

Sax (1989) suggests that whether tests represent an invasion of privacy depends on how they are used. He believes that there is no invasion of privacy when prospective adult test-takers are told how the test will be used and then volunteer to take the test.

When students are involved, Sax (1989) suggests that invasion of privacy issues become more complex. Legally, the schools function *in loco parentis*. Specifically, professional educators are substitutes for parents or legal guardians while students are in school. Acknowledging this function, Sax believes that teachers can require students to take tests as long as tests are not arbitrary, unreasonable, or otherwise illegal.

Sax (1989, Chapter 2) provides an excellent recommendation that principals can use in their schools to protect against invasion of privacy. He recommends that decisions requiring students to take tests (especially personality and attitude assessments) might best be made by a panel including concerned citizens and professional educators knowledgeable about testing. For each test, the panel should

- Determine the capability of the test to measure the objectives the school intends to measure.
- Determine the risk of embarrassing or emotionally damaging students who take the test.
- Assess the acceptability of the test in terms of community values.
- Evaluate the potential benefits of using the test.
- Decide whether the test should be required for all students or only student volunteers.
- Specify how confidentiality of test scores will be ensured.

♦ Investigate the possibility of using appropriate archival data that would eliminate the need for testing.

The *teacher as researcher* is now a popular practice in many
schools. Principals often endorse this practice because they believe that the findings from a well-designed teacher-researcher
project can provide meaningful evaluation information for their
school. In these instances, principals should become familiar
early on with a teacher's proposed research project and be certain that the project plans meet all legal requirements. For example, a teacher-researcher who plans to administer student tests
solely to gather data for a graduate school paper, thesis, or dis-
sertation may very well be violating the legal rights of students
to privacy unless the teacher-researcher obtains the informed
consent of students, their parents or legal guardians, and school
officials.

Question 13. What ethical considerations
should govern the use of tests in the schools?

In reflecting on your response to this question, three important ideas should be kept in mind.

First, recognize that ethical issues are closely related to professional standards and, indeed, often cannot be separated from
them. In professional communities, the solution to this problem
is a set of agreed upon ethical norms (standards) that professionals can use to guide practice.

Second, it is helpful to define who are the test users. Worth-
en, Borg, and White (1993) provide a simple but very helpful
definition: a test user is anyone who selects tests, interprets test
scores, or makes decisions based on test results.

Third, professional associations such as the American Psychological Association (see APA, 1993) have developed and revised over the years a general set of ethical and professional
standards to ensure that tests and assessments are used appropriately, effectively, and fairly. Also available to the education
community is a more specific set of ethical and professional
standards (American Educational Research Association, 1985)
for evaluating the quality of educational tests and assessments,
and for judging the effectiveness and fairness of tests in specific

situations. These educational standards are discussed in all of the educational tests and measurement sources referenced in this chapter.

While principals and their professional colleagues in the schools should be knowledgeable in this area, detailed coverage of one or more of these excellent sources is beyond the scope of this chapter. What is offered below is just a brief overview of some of the more relevant ideas that we have extracted from these sources. These ideas will help you (if needed) formulate a focused self-study plan. We expect that many of these ideas are included in your own self-appraisal response to this question.

SELECTING TESTS. The ethics of responsible test selection require principals and other professional colleagues who select tests to be competent to judge the technical quality of the test and to evaluate the adequacy of supporting materials for effectively administering, scoring, interpreting, and using test results.

Those who select tests for use in the schools must also be competent to judge the procedures used by test developers to make tests as fair as possible for test-takers of different races, gender, ethnic backgrounds, and handicapping conditions.

The principal is often seen as the primary change agent for major changes in the schools. For example, school districts are now continuously revising and improving their inclusion policies to educate students with disabilities (to the maximum extent possible) in regular (general) education classes. In such situations, principals are expected to share the responsibility for ensuring that tests selected for current use have appropriately modified test formats and administration procedures, and are available for test-takers with handicapping conditions

INTERPRETING TEST SCORES. Those who score and interpret test results should have the same technical skills and knowledge expected for those who select tests. This proficiency should include the ability to select and apply the correct norms for the student population of interest, and to prepare reports in formats that communicate accurate interpretations of test findings to the intended audience. These report formats will be different for different audiences. For example, two different types of test score reports would be prepared for a parent conference and for a school district's program evaluation committee.

USING TEST RESULTS. Those who plan to make decisions based on test results are usually not expected to have the same technical competence as those who select tests and interpret test scores. Decision-making competence is of a more general nature. It includes:

- A general, rather than a technical (psychometric) understanding of basic measurement concepts and principles;
- An essential understanding of the issues that surround the limits of tests and test interpretations;
- A clear knowledge about the purposes and actual consequences associated with test use; and
- An informed perspective regarding unethical, illegal, and otherwise inappropriate use of test results in decision making.

Principals and others responsible for planning how test results will be collected and used in decision-making situations should strive to ensure that all involved are knowledgeable about the *actual* tests used in their schools. These responsibilities include ensuring that:

- Test-takers are advised before testing about the purpose and use of the test;
- Test security procedures are in place prior to testing;
- Test-takers are not exposed to coercion or competition as a means to raise test scores; and
- School personnel do not threaten test-takers either with the use of tests or by other unethical strategies that can unrealistically increase the examinees' anxiety about the test.

When the focus of planning shifts from gathering test information toward the actual use of test results, principals and other responsible agents in the schools should strive to ensure that:

♦ Procedural guidelines are in place in the school for communicating a student's test results to parents or legal guardians. These guidelines should include procedures for *describing* what the test measures, *explaining* the meaning of test scores, *clarifying* the accuracy of test scores and *discussing* the use of test results.

♦ Procedural guidelines are in place in the school for keeping a student's test scores confidential among school professionals, the student, and the student's parents or legal guardians. These guidelines should require written consent from the student's parents or guardians before disclosing a student's record to a third party.

♦ Procedural guidelines are available in the school to allow parents and guardians to challenge the accuracy of testing information kept in their children's records. It is also important that these guidelines guarantee students who have reached the age of 18 the same rights formerly granted to their parents or legal guardians.

♦ Procedural guidelines are available in the school to avoid using published test results to assign course grades, or as the sole basis for assignments to remedial programs or retention in grade. While published tests can serve a number of useful purposes, they are not closely enough related to the instructional objectives of particular courses and they typically measure too limited a sample of the intended learning outcomes to be useful for these specific decisions.

Reflecting on the guidelines offered above, it is important to realize that failure to maintain strict confidence of student test results is not only a serious ethical violation but is also illegal. Sax (1989) provides three specific student situations that are exceptions to the violation of strict confidentiality:

♦ When test results uncover a clear and immediate danger to either a student or to others, school officials may advise other professionals in the community or appropriate authorities about this danger;

♦ School officials can share a student's test results with other professionals when they are convinced that sharing these results would be of significant help to the student;

♦ School officials can share test results when a student waives the right to maintain confidentiality.

Program evaluation is seen by many policymakers and practitioners as holding more promise than other (often less formal) approaches for providing schools and school districts with accurate and timely information needed to improve teaching, learning, and school management. For this reason, many schools and school districts are now actively engaged in evaluation studies.

When evaluation studies are used in practice, principals and other professional school colleagues who share responsibility for planning these evaluation studies should strive to ensure that:

♦ Procedural guidelines are available in the schools for finding an ethical compromise between the *need* to use relevant testing and assessment information in evaluation studies and the individual's *right* to personal privacy and freedom of choice. This compromise is best achieved when guidelines guarantee that student anonymity is protected in all published reports.

♦ Procedural guidelines are in place in the school for involving all legitimate evaluation audiences prior to designing the inquiry so that their questions and information needs can be used in determining what new and archival student data must be assembled for data analysis. Focusing evaluation studies to meet just the needs of powerful groups and those who provide the necessary resources for conducting the study are not viewed to be *best practice* because they deliberately ignore many stakeholder groups who are directly affected by the evaluation and who are very likely to have somewhat different information needs and concerns.

♦ Procedural guidelines are available in the school for informing all legitimate evaluation audiences how they can get a complete copy of all published evaluation study reports produced in the school district. Best practice would identify these audiences before an evaluation study is conducted, and at the same time allocate the resources needed for meeting these evaluation report distribution requirements.

Our response to this question on ethical considerations emphasizes that both individuals and their organization share responsibility for ethical use of tests and other assessments. With this in mind, we recommend that all educational professionals be knowledgeable regarding their school districts' published policy position on testing and the use of test information. We also encourage the reader to review the standards for program evaluation which were elaborated earlier in Chapter 2.

CONSTRUCTING NEW MEASURES

Whenever possible, principals should use relevant archival data to inform evaluation and decision making. However, data already available in the schools do not always provide the information that principals and their colleagues need to complete a specific evaluation study. When this situation arises, new measures must be constructed. The required new measures can be qualitative, quantitative, or both.

This section of the self-appraisal system is designed to focus on two essential characteristics needed to construct new measures that yield accurate and relevant evaluation data. These two characteristics are explored first in terms of constructing quantitative measures (focusing on validity and reliability) and then on qualitative measures (focusing on credibility and dependability).

Two ideas are helpful for preparing your personal responses in this section. First, you can bypass the more theoretical research design and philosophical differences between qualitative and quantitative measures by using this obvious distinction.

Think of quantitative measures as data collection devices that use predetermined response categories to present results in numerical form. Similarly, think of qualitative measures as data-collection strategies that observers use to record behaviors as they occur naturally in noncontrived situations. Rather than using numerical counts, the data in qualitative inquiries are presented in the form of rich verbal descriptions that help us uncover actual patterns and relationships in a particular context of interest.

Second, it is usually helpful to view quantitative and qualitative research strategies as complementary rather than competing ways to gather useful information. Along these lines, Erlandson, Harris, Skipper, and Allen (1993) have pointed out that it is useful to recognize that both qualitative and quantitative research studies can be used in *discovery* and *verification*, the two traditional foci for scientific inquiry.

> **Question 14. In quantitative inquiries, two essential characteristics for constructing new measures are validity and reliability. What is the distinction between these two essential characteristics?**

This common distinction can be found in any research methods or evaluation text. Borg, Gall, and Gall (1993) provide this explanation for educational practitioners.

Reliability refers to the degree to which an educational measure yields *consistent* results. For example, reliability is high when two or more observers are in agreement about a common observation or when a student earns a certain score on a test one day and an identical score on the same test on a different day. In more general terms, reliability is the degree to which educational measures are consistent, dependable, or repeatable. The higher the reliability for a measure of interest, the more likely it is free of measurement error.

Validity refers to the extent to which an instrument measures what it claims to measure and, consequently, permits appropriate interpretations. When we refer to the validity of an educational measure, we are usually discussing whether we can use the results as *intended*. In more theoretical terms, validity is the degree to which a certain inference from a test or observation is appropriate and meaningful.

A common misconception is that an educational measure *is* or *is not* valid. An educational measure is not intrinsically valid. It is valid for a particular intent and a particular group. Thus, the question is not whether a measure is valid but, rather, whether it is valid for this purpose and for this person.

With these two descriptions in place, the distinction should be clear. Reliability deals with *consistency*. Validity deals with *intent*. Two additional insights into the distinction follow.

First, the reliability (consistency) of an educational measure is needed to obtain valid results. However, we can have reliability without validity. That is, we can have consistent measures that provide wrong information or are interpreted inappropriately. Thus, reliability is a necessary but not sufficient condition for validity.

Second, the validity (intent) of an educational measure is always specific to some particular use or interpretation. Validity is a matter of degree. It is best considered in terms of categories such as high validity, moderate validity, and low validity. Most important, an educational measure can have high validity *only* when it has high reliability (confidence that errors of measurement are minimized or eliminated). Thus, while we can have high reliability without validity, we cannot have high validity without high reliability.

> **Question 15. Three common measurement procedures used to ensure confidence in the validity of a new quantitative measure are *content validity, concurrent validity,* and *predictive validity*. How would you describe these three measurement procedures and how might they be used in the schools?**

The response to this question uses illustrations from test construction. However, the reader should keep in mind that the validity information shared here has direct application for constructing all forms of new quantitative measures, including closed-end questionnaire items, assessment instruments that use precoded answer categories, and direct observation checklists that require trained observers to count the frequency of specific, clearly defined behaviors.

CONTENT VALIDITY. A test has content validity to the extent that its items represent the content that the test is designed to measure. For example, assume that a test-selection committee in a specific high school decided to use the ABC Algebra Achievement Test to evaluate what students have learned in Algebra I classes this school year. This test would have content validity if the committee can demonstrate that it measures what students were taught in their actual algebra classes.

In the schools, principals and teachers often extend the general interest in content-related validities to include both *curricular validity* (the consistency of test content with curriculum materials) and *instructional validity* (the consistency of test content with what students have been taught). The direct relevance of these two content validity issues for constructing and interpreting teacher-made achievement tests is given in Oosterhoff (1990).

CONCURRENT VALIDITY. A test has concurrent validity to the extent that students' scores on this test (usually a new test under construction or a promising alternative test) correspond to their scores on a known valid test of the same constructs.

Borg, Gall, and Gall (1993) note that concurrent validity studies are often conducted in the schools to locate easy-to-use tests that can be administered in place of complex and expensive tests. They provide this example: Assume that elementary school student scores on a short group-administered test correlated well with their scores on a lengthy individually administered test covering the same content. We would conclude that the brief test has good concurrent validity with the long test. Accordingly, substituting the short test for the long test could yield substantial savings in time and money dedicated to testing.

PREDICTIVE VALIDITY. A test has predictive validity to the extent that scores on the test predict students' future performance on another criterion measure.

Walsh and Betz (1995) offer this example: If we predict that Scholastic Aptitude Test (SAT) scores in high school should be related to grades in college, the correlation between the SAT score and the grade-point average (GPA) is an indicator of predictive validity. Accordingly, if the correlation is zero or in a direction other than that predicted, the predictive validity of the SAT is doubtful. On the other hand, if the correlation is in the direction predicted and its magnitude approaches one, the SAT has high predictive validity for forecasting future performance in college.

The common method of determining a test's predictive validity is to administer the test to a group of students, wait until the behavior that the test claims to predict occurs, and then assess the degree of the relationship between the occurrence of the behavior and the students' scores on the initial test.

Following this standard procedure, elementary school principals could use archival data to verify the predictive validity for reading readiness tests used in their schools. Similarly, high school principals could use archival data to verify the predictive validity of Algebra I readiness tests currently used in their schools to counsel students regarding course selection decisions and the need to get tutorial assistance. Realistically speaking, conducting an actual predictive validity study would probably require the principal to secure some technical assistance from either a counselor or other school district testing expert.

> **Question 16. Three common measurement procedures used to ensure confidence in the reliability of a new quantitative measure are *split-half reliability*, *parallel-form reliability*, and *test-retest reliability*. How would you describe these three measurement procedures and how might they be used in the schools?**

The response to this question also uses illustrations from test construction. As in the previous question, the reader should keep in mind that the reliability information shared here has direct application for constructing all forms of new quantitative measures.

Thinking specifically in terms of reliability, two essential ideas are needed to frame a clear and accurate answer to this question. First, it is important to recall that a test is reliable to the extent that it is free from measurement error. Second, it is critical to recognize that each of these three common reliability procedures focuses on a different type of measurement error. Moreover, each type of measurement error can cause a test to yield inconsistent results.

SPLIT-HALF RELIABILITY. One type of measurement error is caused by inconsistencies in the set of items used in a test. Split-half reliability addresses this problem by providing a method to evaluate the extent to which all items in a test are measuring the same dimension or characteristic.

Split-half reliability inquiries begin by administering a whole test. Next, the test is divided into two comparable halves and separate scores are computed for each half. If student scores obtained from one half of the test are similar to those obtained for the other half, we are reasonably certain the test items are measuring the same construct. When this occurs, we say that the test is *internally consistent*.

Walsh and Betz (1995) suggest that a common approach to split-half test division is to assign the odd-numbered items to one half and the even-numbered items to the other half. In other cases, they recommend that item assignment may be accomplished using a random number table.

Principals should recognize that the split-half approach is a relatively simple but powerful reliability procedure that can be used in the development of teacher-made tests or in the construction of survey questionnaires that their site-based management team might use in program evaluation.

PARALLEL-FORM RELIABILITY. A second type of measurement error occurs when two forms of a test have the same intent and the same number of items, but the items differ in content and style. Parallel-form reliability addresses this problem by providing a method to evaluate the extent to which two different forms of the same test yield similar results. Keep in mind that some measurement books use the term *alternate-form reli-*

ability rather than parallel-form reliability to describe this method.

Parallel-form reliability inquiries require the development of two forms of the test with the assumption that the two forms are measuring the same content or attribute. These two alternate forms, usually designated as Form A and Form B, are administered to a single group of examinees. If scores on Form A are not systematically higher or lower than the scores on Form B, we are reasonably certain that the two tests are measuring the same construct. When this occurs, we say that the two tests are *equivalent.*

Walsh and Betz (1995) suggest that care should be taken to ensure that the two forms contain the same number and type of items. In constructing tests of ability and achievement, the two tests should also be equal in difficulty. Walsh and Betz also recommend that the order in which the two forms are administered should be counterbalanced. This implies that half of the examinees should receive Form A first and the other half should receive Form B first. Counterbalancing is a control for the possible occurrence of fatigue, practice or motivational effects on the test scores.

Principals and their colleagues should recognize that the availability of parallel-form tests in the schools is desirable for several reasons. Specifically, parallel-form tests can be used in program evaluation where before-instruction (beginning of the year) and after-instruction (end of the year) measurements are needed. Using parallel-form tests in this situation ensures that learning gains are the direct result of instruction and that the test scores are not reflecting differences due to student memory of specific test items or other pretest sensitivity issues. Clearly, this claim cannot be made when the same test form is readministered after instruction is completed.

Availability of parallel-form tests serves other purposes as well. They can be used to reassess an individual student when there is some doubt about a specific test result. The use of parallel-form tests also provides a means to reduce the possibility of coaching (teaching to the test) and student cheating.

Because of the time and expense involved in constructing comparable tests, parallel-form reliability is seldom used to construct teacher-made tests. However, the other two reliability procedures treated here can be recommended for this purpose. They are more practical options for teachers, primarily because they require only one test form.

TEST-RETEST RELIABILITY. A third type of measurement error occurs when the students being tested vary their performance from one testing occasion to another. Test-retest reliability addresses this problem by providing a method to evaluate the extent to which scores are consistent (do not fluctuate) when retaking the same test.

Test-retest reliability inquiries involve two administrations of the same test to the same individuals with a time interval separating the two testing sessions. If test scores do not fluctuate, we have a basis for believing that the test is measuring the construct of interest in a consistent and generalized manner across time. When this occurs, we say that the test has *stability*.

Walsh and Betz (1995) recommend a typical time interval of at least one week between test and retest. They also suggest that a retest procedure is appropriate only to the extent that the construct to be measured is assumed to be relatively stable. For example, they believe that intelligence is a stable characteristic and mood states (certain attitudes and predispositions) are not because they are likely to vary considerably over time.

Principals should recognize that test-retest and split-half methods are both useful reliability procedures for constructing most teacher-made tests. Grunlund and Linn (1990) indicated that this is true because teacher-made tests are usually *power tests* (designed to measure performance with ample time conditions) rather than *speed tests* (such as standardized tests that prevent all students from attempting every item). However, considering these two reliability procedures, only the test-retest method should be used to determine the reliability of a teacher-made test if speed is a significant factor.

> **Question 17. In qualitative inquiries, two essential characteristics for constructing and interpreting new measures are *credibility* and *dependability*. What is the distinction between these two essential characteristics?**

Answers to the next three questions, which deal with qualitative inquiries, draw extensively from Erlandson, Harris, Skipper, and Allen (1993). Their guiding principles for conducting qualitative inquiries are based on the *naturalistic inquiry* research paradigm.

Following the theoretical work of Lincoln and Guba (1985), who developed the naturalistic paradigm, Erlandson and his colleagues suggest that the research paradigm operates on this idea: Valid inquiry "must demonstrate its truth value, provide a basis for applying it, and allow for external judgments to be made about the consistency of its procedures and the neutrality of its findings or decisions" (p. 29). Moreover, they note that, taken collectively, these qualities (characteristics of valid inquiry) are called *trustworthiness* in the naturalistic inquiry paradigm.

The two characteristics of trustworthiness addressed in this question are *credibility* and *dependability*. Both concepts are described below. More specific insights into how these concepts are used in the naturalistic paradigm to assess and strengthen qualitative inquiry are explored in the responses to the next two questions.

Credibility in a naturalistic inquiry is the compatibility that exists in the minds of the inquiry's respondents with the research findings that are attributed to them. A qualitative research report achieves credibility to the extent that it communicates the various constructions of reality in a particular setting back to persons who hold them, in a form that will be affirmed by them. Thus, credibility provides evidence to answer this question: *Will each individual respondent in the study acknowledge that the observer's findings represent their specific views of the context under study?*

Dependability in a naturalistic inquiry is the extent to which the inquiry meets the criteria of consistency. Dependability provides evidence to answer this question: *If the inquiry were replicated with the same or similar respondents (participants in the inquiry) in the same or similar setting, would its findings be repeated?*

The distinction in these two terms is this: Credibility deals with the confidence in the accuracy of findings, whereas dependability deals with the consistency in the findings. As two essential characteristics of trustworthiness, these distinct concepts contribute to the methodological adequacy of a qualitative inquiry that permits the researcher to make valid claims to methodological safeguards that parallel those established for quantitative inquiry.

> **Question 18.** *Prolonged engagement, persistent observation, triangulation, referential adequacy materials, peer debriefing* **and** *member checks* **are six strategies used to ensure credibility in qualitative inquiries. How would you describe these six strategies?**

Erlandson, Harris, Skipper, and Allen (1993) argue that data collection and data analysis in qualitative inquiry is a *continuous process.* While the researchers may use a variety of instruments to gather data over time, Erlandson and his colleagues argue that the primary research instrument in qualitative inquiry is the *researcher.* In more specific terms they note that "relying on all its senses, intuition, thoughts and feelings, the human instrument can be a very potent and perceptive data-gathering tool" (p. 82).

Erlandson and his colleagues provide six specific strategies that researchers can use to establish credibility in the continuous process of collecting and analyzing data in qualitative inquiry. These are summarized below.

PROLONGED ENGAGEMENT. Researchers must spend enough time in the context to be studied to overcome the distortions that are due to their impact on the context, their own biases, and the effects of unusual or periodic (seasonal) events. While no exact rules hold here, sufficient time in a context is usually deemed to be the amount of time that the researcher needs to accurately understand daily events in the way the persons who reside in that culture interpret them.

PERSISTENT OBSERVATION. This strategy helps the researcher separate relevancies from irrelevancies and determine when the atypical case is important. A focus on persistent observation is an essential part of credibility because it helps to avoid premature closure of an investigation and, equally important, endorsing too soon an interpretation that is likely to yield an inappropriate conclusion.

TRIANGULATION. This strategy guards against distortions by seeking several different types of sources that can provide insights about the same events or relationships. For example, if a principal reports in an interview that school attendance has dropped significantly over the past two years, the researchers can review attendance documents to verify the accuracy of the principal's statement. In general, triangulation helps establish that information gathered is generally either supported or unconfirmed.

REFERENTIAL ADEQUACY MATERIALS. Because all data must be interpreted in terms of their context, qualitative researchers are encouraged to use a wide array of referential adequacy materials such as videotapes, photographs, tape recordings, brochures, memos, correspondence addressed to teachers, school yearbooks, and other materials that can help the researcher better understand the context of an organization. Credibility of a final report can also be enhanced by sharing such materials in report briefing sessions for stakeholders and other researchers.

PEER DEBRIEFING. This strategy helps the researcher build credibility by using professionals from *outside* the organization under study to debrief the researcher and to provide insights that refine and, in some cases, redirect the inquiry process.

MEMBER CHECKS. This strategy helps the researcher build credibility by using members from *inside* the organization to test the researcher's categories (developed in content analysis), subsequent interpretations (based on linking categories), and the overall conclusions (emerging from this process). Qualitative researchers almost always believe this strategy to be the most important for establishing credibility because it provides members of the organization being studied several opportunities during the inquiry to indicate whether the reconstructions of the researcher are recognizable.

Question 19. Creating an audit trail and using a reflexive journal are two strategies used to en-

sure dependability in qualitative inquiries. How would you describe these two strategies?

Erlandson, Harris, Skipper, and Allen (1993) provide two specific strategies researchers can use to establish dependability in qualitative inquiry. Keep in mind that dependability addresses the criterion of consistency, which assumes that replication of designated procedures will not yield different results.

DEPENDABILITY AUDIT. To provide for a check on dependability, the researcher must make it possible for an *external check* to be conducted on the process by which the study was conducted. Erlandson and his colleagues (1993) note that this is accomplished in qualitative inquiry by providing an *audit trail* that includes six basic types of auditing materials: raw data; data reduction and analysis products; data reconstruction and synthesis products; process notes; materials relating to intentions and dispositions; and information relative to any instrument development (see Chapter 7 for more specific details).

REFLEXIVE JOURNAL. This type of journal is usually described as a kind of diary that a qualitative researcher keeps on a regular basis to record relevant information regarding the researcher's schedule and logistics, insights, and reasons for methodological decisions. Researchers often word process entries in their journal on a weekly basis. A printout of the computerized journal becomes a part of the audit trail for the study.

In some qualitative inquiries, researchers use tape recorders on a daily basis to verbalize their thoughts, working hypotheses, unanswered questions, uncertainties, and ideas for further refinement of data collection strategies. These daily recordings can then be used to construct weekly entries in their word processing files. In addition to building an accurate computerized audit trail, this process prepares the researcher for data collection to be undertaken in subsequent weeks of the study.

Two practical suggestions for further study are recommended for this section of the self-appraisal. Beginning researchers interested in conducting qualitative research studies can find both practical suggestions and references to a wide variety of other sources covering qualitative methods in Erlandson, Harris, Skipper, and Allen (1993).

Those interested in comparing and contrasting the specific characteristics of qualitative and quantitative inquiries might begin by examining three basic sources. McNamara and McNamara (1995a) discuss how these two forms of inquiry can both be used to improve school public relations. Two excellent educational research methods texts that have been substantially revised to reflect a balance of both qualitative and quantitative research methods are Gall, Borg, and Gall (1996) and McMillan and Schumacher (1993). These two texts are well within the grasp of a beginning researcher.

CLASSIFYING MEASUREMENT INSTRUMENTS

Our purpose in this section of the self-appraisal is to explore your understanding of how educational and psychological measurements can be classified. Personal responses to the questions offered here, followed by your analysis of our responses to the same questions, should help you impose some order on the wide array of tests and other measures currently used in the schools.

Question 20. In your own words, describe and classify the measurement instruments that you have encountered in your professional work?

Worthen, Borg, and White (1993, Chapter 4) note that every measurement text has its preferred way of describing and classifying educational and psychological tests. For comparative purposes, here is a summary of their thirteen-category classification system. Tests and other measurement instruments can be classified:

BY SUBJECT AREA OF DISCIPLINE. This category describes a test by indicating the area or discipline measured. Using this category, we describe tests as reading tests, mathematics tests, or music tests, or, if they cut across disciplines, we may think of a science test as an instrument that samples a student's knowledge in biology, chemistry, and physics.

BY PSYCHOLOGICAL CONSTRUCT. This category defines tests in terms of the psychological construct measured. Here tests are described as intelligence tests, attitude tests, achievement tests, vocational interest tests, and so forth.

BY SPECIFIC SKILLS OR BEHAVIORS. A somewhat more specific distinction for classifying tests lets one describe tests by the skills and behaviors they require. If a test requires reading, speaking, or writing skills, it is a verbal test. Similarly, if it requires working with numerical skills, it is a nonverbal or quantitative test.

BY ITEM FORMAT. While all tests do not have items per se, tests can be easily classified by format. For this classification, Worthen, Borg, and White (1993, p. 70) offer these examples:

- ♦ Essay Tests (items requiring verbal responses)
- ♦ Completion Tests (examinee provides either fill-in-the-blank or short answers to direct questions)
- ♦ Multiple-Choice Tests (items requiring students to select one of many possible answers)
- ♦ True-False Tests (statements that examinees declare to be correct or incorrect)
- ♦ Matching Tests (items requiring students to correctly match terms or concepts)
- ♦ Rating Scales (items requiring students to rate concerns of interest)

BY TYPE OF DATA PRODUCED. Tests are often classified as quantitative or qualitative depending on the data they collect.

BY THE PURPOSE FOR WHICH THEY ARE USED. Using the purpose for which they are administered allows tests to be classified as diagnostic tests, placement tests, job application tests, admission tests, licensing tests, certification tests, and so on.

BY HOW THE TEST IS ADMINISTERED. The most common distinction for this category is between *individually* administered tests and *group* tests. For example, most intelligence tests are individual tests administered by counselors or psychologists. Most achievement tests are group tests administered by teachers.

BY HOW THE TEST IS SCORED. This category typically describes tests as either *objective* (cases where scorers readily agree about what is a correct response) or *subjective* (cases where scorers do not always agree on what constitutes a correct response).

Multiple-choice, true-false, and matching tests are usually objective tests. Essay examinations are subjective tests.

BY THE TYPE OF PERFORMANCE REQUIRED. This category is used to classify a test in terms of measuring either *typical performance* (often accomplished by using power tests that allow students to respond to each item) or *maximum performance* (often accomplished by using speed tests that have strict time limits). Most teacher-made tests and quizzes used in classrooms are power tests.

BY WAYS OF RECORDING BEHAVIOR. Another specific way to classify tests is based on how behavioral measures are recorded. Worthen, Borg, and White (1993, p. 72) offer these classification examples:

♦ Mechanical Devices (using tape recorders)
♦ Independent Observers (applying checklists)
♦ Interviews (conducting telephone surveys)
♦ Student Self-Reports (completing a questionnaire)
♦ Student Personal Products (submitting samples of work)
♦ Unobtrusive Instruments (using a hidden camera)

BY TYPES OF OBJECTIVES MEASURED. Tests can be classified using different educational objectives. The most common way to use this category is to classify tests as *cognitive tests* (dealing with thinking, knowing, and problem-solving), *affective tests* (dealing with attitudes, interests, and values), and *psychomotor tests* (measuring manual and motor skills).

BY HOW THE SCORE IS INTERPRETED. One of the most important ways to describe different types of tests is by how the score is interpreted. For example, achievement tests are commonly classified as either norm-referenced tests or criterion-referenced tests.

A *norm-referenced test* is an objective test whose scores are interpreted relative to the performance of other individuals in a defined group. A *criterion-referenced test* is an objective test whose scores are interpreted relative to some absolute performance standard. Strictly speaking, the fundamental distinction between criterion-referencing and norm-referencing is a matter of how scores are interpreted rather than the type of testing instrument used. Moreover, some testing experts acknowledge that scores from any test can be interpreted in either a criterion-referenced manner or in a norm-referenced manner. For these reasons, test experts often use the terms norm-referenced tests and criterion-referenced tests for convenience and consistency across test-user groups, but when they are challenged, they are quick to point out that their actual reference is only to score interpretation.

BY WHO CONSTRUCTS THEM AND HOW. Tests are often classified by the manner in which they were constructed and by the professional who constructs them. Standardized tests and teacher-made tests are the most common designations used to describe tests in this classification category.

A *standardized test* is usually constructed by a professional test developer. A standardized test is a test for which formal procedures have been developed to ensure consistency in the administration and scoring across all testing situations. It is helpful to note here that both norm-referenced and criterion-referenced tests can be standardized. Moreover, publishers of standardized tests usually provide norms that yield percentile ranks and grade-equivalent scores for test-users to compare an individual student's score with those of other students on relevant characteristics.

A *teacher-made test* is a test constructed by a teacher to test students in that teacher's classroom. Teacher-made tests come in many forms. In addition to the classifications elaborated above, conditions for taking teacher-made tests include contrasting procedures, such as open-book versus closed-book tests and in-class versus take-home examinations.

Keep in mind that the thirteen ways that Worthen, Borg, and White (1993) specified to classify tests are not independent. For example, thinking in terms of the different classification options within the category *by item format*, recognize that it is very possible to have a single test that uses multiple-choice, matching, short answer, and essay formats. Worthen, Borg, and White (1993) illustrate the interdependence of these categories by showing how they described a single test using all thirteen classification dimensions. They also note that measurement texts and yearbooks present critiques of tests using several of the thirteen classifications for each test reviewed.

More extensive coverage of the measurement characteristics identified in this response is beyond the scope of this chapter. However, one additional question is offered to focus on the potential of recently proposed alternatives to standardized testing.

Question 21. What are alternative assessments?

On the job and in university classrooms, we frequently encounter terms such as *authentic assessment, direct assessment,* and *performance assessment.* The generic term often used to cover these labels is *alternative assessment.*

Worthen, Borg, and White (1993, Chapter 15) note that these terms reflect subtle distinction in emphasis, while sharing two essential commonalties. First, they are all seen as *alternatives* to traditional achievement tests that use multiple-choice test items. Second, they all deal with direct examination of student performance on meaningful tasks relevant to life outside of school.

Proponents of alternative assessments prefer them to more traditional tests that rely only on multiple-choice test items because they believe that student learning can be better assessed by judging a student's actual performance on relevant tasks.

Worthen, Borg, and White (1993, p. 419) argue that alternative or direct assessment of student performance is by no means a new idea in education. They provide these time-honored examples that indicate direct performance assessment on relevant tasks:

- ◆ Language Proficiency Testing (conversations and translations)
- ◆ Competency Testing (for teachers and administrators)
- ◆ Manual Assessments (in drafting and welding)
- ◆ Holistic Student Products (writing portfolios)
- ◆ Portfolios of Student Work (all student products for a unit)
- ◆ Cumulative Student Record Files (archival data)
- ◆ Student Live Performances (in music and athletics)

- Teacher's Anecdotal Records (of student performance)
- Teacher's Checklists (on a student's performance)
- Teacher-Made Achievement Tests (with grades)
- Role-Playing Devices (simulations of a historical event)

While consideration of the many benefits and limitations of alternative assessment is beyond the scope of this book, it is helpful to reference three central ideas put forth by experts in this area. First, classroom teachers are the gatekeepers of effective alternative assessment. Second, there is currently little agreement about the exact criteria to be used to determine the quality of alternative forms of assessment. Third, not all stakeholders, such as legislators, school boards, parents, and members of professional associations, readily accept the importance and usefulness of alternative assessment, especially as an accountability device to either replace or extend standardized achievement testing.

Two recommendations for further study regarding alternative assessments in the schools deserve mention here. A condensed but excellent comprehensive treatment of issues and concerns is Worthen, Borg, and White (1993), whose Chapter 15 is appropriately entitled *Avoiding Being Caught in the Crossfire between Standardized Test Supporters and Alternative Assessment Enthusiasts*. Four recent paperbacks that principals can provide to begin a campus professional development library for their teachers in this area are Airasian (1996), Gallagher (1998), Gronlund (1998), and Stiggins (1997). Each deals with the development of classroom tests and provided us relevant practical insights for preparing this chapter. Two additional sources for this library are Johnson (1996a, 1996b).

INTERVIEWS AND DIRECT OBSERVATION

Interviews and direct observation are frequently used in qualitative inquiries. In these situations, data collection and analysis should be guided by the strategies that are used to ensure both credibility and dependability. These two characteristics of qualitative inquiry were addressed earlier in the chapter.

Using a consumer of research perspective, this section focuses on two general questions that should help when evaluating research studies. The first question focuses on evaluating an inquiry that uses interviews to collect data in a school program evaluation project. The second question focuses on evaluating a study where an instructional supervisor in a school is expected to observe and count clearly defined teacher behaviors elaborated in a standardized teacher observation checklist.

> **Question 22. A principal in your school district asks you to evaluate an action research project that was just completed in her school. This inquiry used interviews to collect all relevant data. What general guidelines would you specify to help you evaluate this campus research project?**

Borg, Gall, and Gall (1993, Chapter 6) provide six general guidelines to help reviewers evaluate research studies that use interviews to collect data. Their six guidelines are stated as questions. Responses offered below for the six guiding questions reflect the perspectives provided by Borg and his colleagues.

♦ How well were the interviewers trained?

The level of training required for interviewers is directly related to the type of information needed and the time allocated to collect it. Reviewers should keep in mind that a well-trained interviewer has the skills needed to alter the interview situation at any time to obtain the best possible responses from interviewees within realistic time constraints.

♦ How was information recorded?

Some research experts claim that audiotaping (when permitted) is preferred to having interviewers take notes. They argue that audiotaping provides accurate interview data that helps to reduce potential bias due to preconceived ideas or cases where interviewers might not record responses that disagree with their beliefs.

♦ How much judgment was called for?

Interviews can be structured, semistructured, or unstructured. In educational research, interviews are usually semistructured. For this type of study, interview guides (checklists detailing all semistructured questions and the relevant procedures) should provide interviewers the option to get more information or to clarify the interviewee's responses. Moreover, the interview guide should encourage the interviewer to use these options with all interviewees.

♦ Were the interview procedures tried out before the study began?

A carefully executed pilot study is the best strategy one can use to ensure that safeguards are in place for obtaining accurate and unbiased data. The pilot study should be described in the published research report that presents the findings for the inquiry.

♦ Were leading questions asked?

A leading question is any question whose phrasing leads the interviewee to believe that one response is more desirable than another. Leading questions should be avoided at all costs. The actual questions used in the study should be included in the report so that readers can make their own judgment about the use of leading questions.

♦ How much did the interviewer know about the research?

Some experts believe that interviewers should know as little as possible about the explicit purpose of the study. To accomplish this goal, they recommend that researchers should not serve as interviewers. This strategy is most often applied in large-scale experimental studies, where interviewers do not need to know hypotheses predicting differential outcomes for two or more experimental alternatives, and in collecting basic interview data in national polls.

In ethnographic investigation, naturalistic inquiries, and practical (action-oriented) studies, the researcher is usually responsible for collecting interview data, conducting data analysis, and for preparing research reports. In these situations, research consumers should review research reports to uncover evidence that speaks directly to credibility and dependability (see responses to questions 17 to 19).

Alternative answers providing similar guidelines to evaluate research studies using interviews are available in any basic behavioral science or educational research methods textbook. For example, an up-to-date coverage of interviewing for the beginning behavioral science researcher is given in Leary (1995) and for the educational practitioner in McMillan and Schumaker (1993). Teacher-researchers may also wish to examine the excellent paperback by Eisenhart and Borko (1993).

> **Question 23. A principal in your school district asks you to evaluate a standardized direct observation checklist that the campus committee has developed to gather classroom data for planning staff development activities dealing with effective teaching and student learning. What general guidelines would you identify to help you evaluate this school research project?**

Borg, Gall, and Gall (1993, Chapter 6) provide five general guidelines to help reviewers evaluate research studies that use direct observation instruments to collect data. These five guidelines are stated as questions. Responses offered below for the five guiding questions reflect the perspectives provided by Borg and his colleagues.

♦ Were high-inference or low-inference behaviors observed?

Assume an observer is given a general definition of teacher effectiveness and is then asked to rate the degree to which each teacher is effective on a scale from 1 to 9. In this appraisal procedure, teacher effectiveness is defined as a *high-inference* behavior because the observer must form an overall judgment without reference to specific guidelines or criteria.

Consider an alternate situation where trained observers are asked to count the frequency of specific well-defined teaching strategies that contribute to the overall effectiveness of teaching. Such strategies would include teacher use of advance organizers, student motivators, clear objectives for the lesson, and a review of these objectives at the end of the lesson. In this standardized appraisal system, teacher effectiveness would be classified as a *low-inference* behavior.

This is an important distinction. Specifically, direct observation using a skilled interviewer to rate individuals on a low-inference (well-defined) behavior usually produces very reliable and valid measures for the construct being observed. Direct observation using unskilled observers to rate individuals on a high-inference (abstract) behavior often yields poor reliability and validity measures for the construct being observed. Although some high-inference behaviors can be observed reliably by skilled observers, low-inference behaviors are preferred in most direct observation studies.

> ◆ Were observers trained to identify the variables to be observed?

Each direct observation procedure assumes certain observer skills are in place. If the skills required to use a specific observational procedure exceed the skills observers have to observe the constructs (variables) of interest, training is needed to ensure that observers will produce valid and reliable observations.

Texas law, for example, recently required all principals to use a standardized direct-observation checklist (developed for statewide use) for evaluating all classroom teachers. The law also required all principals to complete a training program (including a certificate provision) that ensured their competency to use this checklist correctly in their schools.

> ◆ Was there interobserver reliability?

Reliability in this case refers to the level of agreement between the observations of independent observers. For standardized procedures, the indicator of interobserver reliability is determined by using a correlation coefficient. For skilled observers, the correlations for interobserver (also called interrater) reliability usually exceed 0.85. These correlation values indicate that the level of agreement for observations taken on the same event or individual is above 85 percent.

♦ How long was the observation period?

The observation should be long enough to yield a representative sample of all relevant behaviors of interest in the inquiry. Shorter observation periods often produce results that are atypical.

While there are no absolute rules, Borg and his colleagues (1993) suggest that "the necessary period of observation will depend on such factors as the nature of the behaviors being observed, the circumstances under which the behavior can occur, and its frequency of occurrence" (p. 118). Thus, the actual length of the observation period for a specific study is always a judgment call.

♦ How conspicuous were the observers?

While university laboratory studies can often use a one-way screen to conceal observers, it is very unlikely that these conditions can be used in practice.

In most field studies, observers need to be visible to individuals being observed for ethical reasons. They must also be aware that their presence is likely to have a direct impact on behaviors being observed. As student-teacher supervisors know all too well, this impact is very likely to happen when they enter the student-teacher's classroom for the first time.

Borg and his colleagues (1993) suggest this problem can be solved to a large extent if a researcher asks the observers not to record any data for the first few minutes after they arrive at the observational site. When teacher-observation checklists are used, the procedures given to observers usually recommend that they not comment on classroom activity during the observational period, nor should they use nonverbal communications to disrupt the typical behavior of the teacher being observed. Both procedures usually help to make observers unobtrusive.

It is a good research practice for observational studies to include a description of the procedures that observers followed to be unobtrusive. When appropriate, these studies should also report estimates to indicate possible effects that can be attributed to the presence of the observer.

Alternative answers providing similar guidelines to evaluate research studies that use direct observation are available in any basic behavioral science or educational research methods text. An excellent second source that you can use to reanalyze your personal response to the hypothetical situation that you were asked to evaluate in this question is Worthen, Borg, and White (1993, Chapter 9).

As we recommended in our response to the previous question dealing with interviews, qualitative research studies that use direct evaluation should be evaluated using the guidelines established for credibility and dependability (see information provided for questions 17 to 19, pp. 111–116).

QUESTIONNAIRE DESIGN AND USE

In their book *Polls and Surveys*, Bradburn and Sudman (1988) argue that scientific survey sampling in the United States began on a regular basis in July 1935 when *Fortune* magazine published the first *Fortune Poll* conducted by Elmo Roper and his colleagues. Later in that same year, George Gallup began a syndicated service to thirty-five newspapers that was soon known everywhere as the *Gallup Poll*.

Today, the findings of surveys and polls (which are interchangeable terms) are now used for many purposes. In general, they serve as aids to planning and decision making in government agencies, educational organizations, political action groups, business corporations, and a wide array of not-for-profit institutions.

Most professional educators are familiar with using surveys to help schools and universities to:

♦ Evaluate the results of promising interventions;

♦ Inform strategic planning;

♦ Assess what is learned in schools;

♦ Predict the need for classroom facilities; and

♦ Monitor the implementation of specific decisions or new procedures.

The three most common survey types are mail surveys, face-to-face interviews, and telephone surveys. While their design features are different (Dillman and Salant, 1994), each of these survey methods use questionnaires to collect data. The two basic building blocks used to construct questionnaires are open-end (qualitative) questions and closed-end (quantitative) questions.

This section of the self-appraisal explores your understanding of questionnaire design and use. It requests answers to four questions. The first three questions deal with constructing questionnaire items. The fourth question focuses on guidelines for publishing survey research findings.

> **Question 24. You have just accepted the invitation to serve as a member of a school district's strategic planning committee that is now designing a needs assessment survey to guide the development of a new five-year plan. At the start of a survey planning session, each member of the committee is asked to construct one open-end and one closed-end questionnaire item. What is your response to this request?**

A *closed-end question* asks respondents to select their own answers from a list provided by the survey researcher. McNamara (1997a) provides the following illustrations that address two basic concerns in strategic planning.

A *report card* question is a quantitative questionnaire item used to get stakeholder opinions about the effectiveness of current programs and services. A sample item is: *Students are often given the grades A, B, C, D, and Fail to denote the quality of their work. Suppose the social studies program in your child's school were graded the same way. What grade would you give the social studies program in your child's school?*

If several report card items were included in the same questionnaire, a one-page school district report card could be constructed to summarize the results for all report card items. An example of a school district report card is given in McNamara (1997a).

A *needs assessment* item is a quantitative questionnaire item used to provide insights for identifying current practices that merit continuation and for creating new organizational efforts that address current needs. A sample item is: *How well do you be-lieve the needs of physically handicapped students are met in your child's school? Are they fully met, adequately met, poorly met, not met at all, or don't know/no opinion?*

If the needs-assessment item-format is used to assess several concerns, a one-page needs assessment profile can be construct-ed to summarize the results for these common items.

An *open-end question* asks respondents to provide their own answers to the question. McNamara (1997a) recommends that three open-end questions should be included in a strategic plan-ning questionnaire:

Question A. In your opinion, in what way is your child's school particularly good?

Question B. What do you think are the three biggest problems with which the public schools in the dis-trict must deal?

Question C. The school district is working on a revised education plan for the next five years. What do you think are the three most important things on which they should work?

While often overlooked in questionnaire design, it is essen-tial that questionnaire items be put in a sequence that minimizes the extent to which only one item can compromise or bias the re-sponse to a subsequent item. For this reason, McNamara (1997a) recommends the following sequence.

The school strengths item *(Question A)* should be the first item in the questionnaire. Using this approach, no other ques-tionnaire item will directly influence a respondent's position on school strengths.

The problems-in-the-schools item *(Question B)* should be placed toward the front of the questionnaire before all closed-end items dealing with needs assessment concerns.

The third open-end item *(Question C)* is saved for last. When this open-end question is used as the final item in the question-naire, it helps remind respondents that their preferences and concerns will be studied by their school district's strategic plan-ning committee.

Question 25. What are the advantages and disadvantages of using open-end questions?

ADVANTAGES. Dillman (1978) suggests that open-end questionnaire items are most often used when survey researchers and policymakers cannot anticipate the various ways in which people are likely to respond to a question. He also notes that open-end questions are used in questionnaires to stimulate free thought, generate suggestions, probe people's memories, and clarify position.

McNamara (1997a) notes that open-end questions give respondents an opportunity to answer in their own words. Other advantages of open-end questionnaire items are that they:

♦ Eliminate the need for several multiple choice questions to cover one issue;

♦ Provide an opportunity for gathering a wide variety of responses on complex issues;

♦ Offer flexibility in creating a questionnaire format;

♦ Allow respondents to express their depth of conviction or feeling;

♦ Allow respondents to express their ambivalence if it exists; and

♦ Provide survey researchers an opportunity to determine the respondent's level of understanding of the question.

DISADVANTAGES. Given these advantages, McNamara notes that practitioners are often inclined to make extensive use of open-end items in their questionnaires. Before practitioners decide to use this strategy in their questionnaire designs, they should first carefully examine the disadvantages of using open-end questions. Five commonly referenced disadvantages of the open-end question format are:

♦ Responses are more time-consuming to record;

♦ Responses are difficult and expensive to code;

♦ Response data are difficult to tabulate and to process into meaningful categories;

♦ Meaningful coding is often difficult and requires a professional-level of knowledge about the topic; and

♦ Coding often requires the survey researcher to interpret the respondent's response for coding or tabulation.

Keep in mind that open-end questionnaire items achieve their intended purpose when the questions are relevant, avoid ambiguous terms, and ask for information that respondents are competent to provide.

Question 26. What are the advantages and disadvantages of using closed-end questions?

ADVANTAGES. Babbie (1990) notes that closed-end questions are very popular in survey research because they provide greater uniformity of responses and are more easily processed. For example, closed-end responses can be marked directly on optical-sensing sheets by the respondents for automatic data entry.

A content analysis of several survey methods texts provided additional advantages. Because answers to closed-end questions yield quantitative responses to predetermined answer categories, they are usually inexpensive to administer, amenable to statistical data analysis with minimal manipulation of the raw data, and allow for the use of a wide variety of statistical procedures.

DISADVANTAGES. Babbie (1990) notes that a major shortcoming of closed-end questions lies in the researcher's structuring of predetermined response categories. Specifically, when survey researchers design the response categories for a given question dealing with *the most important issues* about a policy concern, they might overlook certain issues that respondents would have said were important. Sometimes this problem can be avoided by using pilot tests to ensure that response categories are exhaustive, or by adding a response category *other (please elaborate)*. However, adding the response category *other* does not guarantee that respondents will use this option.

The content analysis referenced above also uncovered these additional limitations:

- Lack of communication between the researcher and the respondent can result in misunderstandings;
- Problems arise related to choosing the right words to convey proper meaning;
- Closed answers allow those who don't know what they are talking about to respond; and
- Equal weight is given in data analysis to all respondents without any means to differentiate between those who understand the topic and those who do not.

Keep in mind that there are benefits and limitations associated with both open-end and closed-end questions. For this reason, many questionnaires are constructed using both types of questions. Most important, readers should never be misled into thinking that there is one *right* way and one *wrong* way to ask questions. Those wishing further information on questionnaire design will find references to the several noteworthy questionnaire design sources in McNamara (1994a).

> **Question 27. Your strategic planning committee is now ready to prepare the final report on the findings of its needs assessment survey. You are asked to provide some guidelines for publishing an accurate disclosure of the research design characteristics used in the survey. How would you respond?**

In all professional fields, there is a clear expectation that survey research practitioners have an ethical obligation to accurately report both the *methods* and the *results* of their survey. To meet these expectations, survey reports should include a discussion of the problems, shortcomings, and negative, as well as positive, findings of the survey.

Because ethical concerns are not part of scientific method, McNamara (1994a) notes that survey research practitioners must look to another set of guidelines. These guidelines are given in the *Code of Professional Ethics and Practices* published by the American Association of Public Opinion Researchers

(AAPOR), an interdisciplinary association of both academic and commercial survey researchers.

AAPOR guidelines indicate that a published survey report should provide an accurate disclosure of these nine research design characteristics:

- ◆ Purpose of the survey (in non-technical terms)
- ◆ Sponsor of the survey (organization or agency)
- ◆ Sample sizes used in data analysis
- ◆ Base of the response (response rate for the sampling plan)
- ◆ Time of the interview (dates data were collected)
- ◆ How respondents were contacted (telephone, mail, etc.)
- ◆ Definition of the target population (inferential base)
- ◆ Exact wording of the questions used in the survey
- ◆ Error allowance (margin of error)

Principals who plan to use surveys in their schools can find several discussions of these AAPOR ethical guidelines as they apply to all survey operations in McNamara (1994a). The last chapter in this book also provides a 100-item checklist that principals can use to plan their survey or to evaluate published survey reports that offer findings for improving instruction and school administration.

Principals who want to construct their own questionnaire may wish to examine the practical approach to building questionnaires given in Cox (1996). This book was prepared with inexperienced and rushed questionnaire writers in mind. Its step-by-step procedures are all explained using a single case-study illustration dealing with leadership of elementary school principals.

Three current case-study articles that illustrate how principals can use graphical methods to communicate their questionnaire design and results to the public are McNamara (1997a, 1997b, and 1998). More general guidelines for preparing visual displays of questionnaire results can be found in the early chapters of most basic statistics texts.

ADMINISTRATIVE DECISION MAKING

The use of archival data and new measures to inform decision making on the job is a central theme in this chapter. The final section of the self-appraisal extends this theme by asking the reader to answer three specific questions dealing with administrative decision making.

Question 28. How would you define administrative decision making?

Herbert Simon is probably best known today as the winner of the 1978 Nobel Prize in Economics. Over the past several decades, both scholars and practitioners have been influenced by his research and writings on administrative decision making and organizational problem solving.

Simon (1977) divides administrative decision making into four principal phases: *intelligence activity*, which consists of searching the environment for occasions (problems) calling for decisions; *design activity*, which centers on inventing, developing, and analyzing courses of action; *choice activity*, which encompasses actually selecting a particular course of action from those available; and *review activity*, which consists of evaluating past choices.

Simon's model clearly implies that an administrator is involved in all stages of decision making, not simply in the act of choice. Generally speaking, Simon's model assumes that intelligence activity precedes design, and design activity precedes choice. However, Simon believes that the cycle is far more complex than this sequence suggests. Yet, he believes that the first three phases in his decision model "are often discernible as the organizational decision process unfolds" (p. 43).

The implications of Simon's model for decision making in educational organizations are reviewed in McNamara (1993). For our purposes, it is important to realize that relevant archival data and new measures can be analyzed to inform administrative decisions that fall into any one of the four phases in Simon's model. Moreover, his theoretical perspectives provide school principals with a means to *reflect* on their own administration decision-making practices and to *analyze* the decision-making strategies they are likely to encounter in their own practicing professional environments. Finally, defining administrative decision making solely in terms of making choices does little to help us think in terms of data-based decision making.

Question 29. Decision theorists frequently make a distinction between data and information. What is implied in this distinction?

Data are facts. Data become information when they are put into a form that speaks directly to the decision issues at hand. Here are three examples of this distinction.

A test statistic is a well-defined statistical procedure that uses *data* to provide *information* to help decide if a hypothesis of interest should be confirmed or rejected.

The Consumer Price Index (CPI) uses monthly *data* on 400 consumer items (data are actual costs for food, clothing, housing, transportation, medical care, and other services) to produce *information* (economic index values) to make decisions that link prices, wages, and taxes to the rate of inflation. To increase the information value of the CPI, the federal government publishes separate indices to assist decision makers in the nation's 28 largest metropolitan areas.

A management information system uses *data* to generate *information* (in the form of custom reports) that helps managers and policymakers decide which aspects of the organization can and should be improved.

Structuring data to yield useful information in administrative decision making does not always depend on using complex mathematical methods or sophisticated computer programs. Decision-oriented information can also be obtained using simple graphic techniques. While often overlooked, many valuable insights can be obtained from data by constructing plots with paper and pencil.

The distinction between data and information is reflected in statements such as *schools are data rich but analysis poor,* or *data without a theoretical framework are meaningless.*

While most practitioners are aware of this distinction, they frequently use the words *data* and *information* interchangeably.

This usage is both for convenience and because other professional colleagues and writers follow this practice.

> **Question 30. You are the principal on a campus that has a school-improvement committee. This committee asks you to provide some guidelines for planning the evaluation of a new instructional program that has operated in the school for the past two years. Assuming you are familiar with the importance of the distinction between data and information, how would you respond to their request?**

Best practice in evaluation uses the distinction between data and information to plan program evaluations. Once an evaluation is deemed an appropriate endeavor, planning is usually undertaken using these three basic steps.

STEP ONE. The initial step is used to assemble all potentially relevant questions offered by stakeholders (individuals and groups affected by the evaluation). Keep in mind that good questions come from many sources. While several questions might appear to be unanswerable, this problem is addressed in a later step.

STEP TWO. The next logical step is to determine what information is needed to answer each question. While this step may appear routine, it is critical. The following chart matrix is a worksheet to complete this step. Columns are used to structure important elements in the evaluation plan. Each row deals with a single question generated in step one. While column headings can vary, here is good column structure:

Column One:	Evaluation Questions
Column Two:	Information Required
Column Three:	Available Data
Column Four:	New Data to Be Collected
Column Five:	Data Collection Method
Column Six:	Arrangements for Collecting Data
Column Seven:	Data Analysis Procedures
Column Eight:	Strategy Used to Reach Conclusion

If Step One produced 35 questions, the worksheet would be a 35×8 matrix. When the eight appropriate entries are inserted for all rows, the evaluation planner has a concise way to study all relevant concerns. Bypassing this step, an evaluation project can be conducted using data, but it will more than likely be implemented without answering critical questions.

STEP THREE. No evaluation can answer all questions stakeholders propose. This step is used to select those questions that provide the most relevant information for the overall purpose of the study. The final list of questions should reflect the ability to answer all top priority questions in a quality manner, and ensure that this list addresses all major concerns of stakeholders.

Put briefly, using this three-step process helps guarantee that all required data are put into a form that speaks directly to decision issues at hand.

An excellent treatment of this three-step planning process and that emphasizes program evaluation in the schools is given in Worthen, Borg, and White (1993). Several data-structuring methods linked to Simon's (1977) four phases of decision making are elaborated in McNamara (1994b) and McNamara, Dickson, and Guido-Dibrito (1988).

SUMMARY

This chapter provided principals and their colleagues with an overview of basic measurement concepts, issues, and strategies that have direct application in the schools using a self-appraisal system that has 30 questions. For your convenience and use, all 30 questions are reprinted in the Appendix. The *comparison* response we constructed for each question in the self-appraisal system includes a direct reference to one or more basic sources that can be explored to get more detailed information. Thus, the appraisal system also provides a useful self-study guide.

Acknowledgments: The initial plans for this chapter profited from insights provided by ten doctoral students who participated in a Spring 1996 seminar on *Measurement and Evaluation in the Schools* conducted in the Texas A&M University Department of Educational Administration by the first two authors. Accordingly, we wish to thank Cynthia Barrett, Fidel Fernandez, Chrissy Hester, Woodrow Jackson, Cindy Locke, Amy Minke, Karin Quenk, Judy Reimer, Lowell Strike, and Nilah Wright. This seminar session also involved multiple telephone conferences with three TAMU doctoral graduates now serving as school principals. For their contributions, we wish to thank again David Bishop, Sandra McCalla, and Jane MacDonald.

ACTION FOLLOW-UP

1. In Chapter 3, you prepared a response indicating new and archival that data you would like to have in order to learn about the potential of the school and your place in it if you assumed this school principalship. Reexamine your response using the measurement concepts, issues, and strategies addressed in this chapter.

2. Design and conduct a predictive validity study for a school using archival data. In an elementary school, your predictor might be a Reading Readiness Test. In a high school, your predictor might be an Algebra I Readiness Test.

3. Secure and evaluate a school district's policy on testing. Use the responses to questions 12 (p. 98) and 13 (p. 99) as a guide to conduct your evaluation.

PART III

APPLICATIONS

6

COLLABORATIVE PROBLEM SOLVING

The origin of all twenty-one books included in the School Leadership Library is a single landmark publication entitled *Principals for Our Changing Schools: Knowledge and Skill Base*. Commissioned by the National Policy Board of Educational Administration (NPBEA) and edited by Scott D. Thomson, this 1993 publication describes a new knowledge and skill base for principals to meet the challenge of practice in the twenty-first century.

Viewed as a new starting point for principal preparation, *Principals for Our Changing Schools* produced a typology consisting of twenty-one domains that constitute what principals must know and be able to do. As indicated in the foreword, the twenty-one domains in this NPBEA typology are not discrete; they are interrelated. Specifically, eleven of these domains (1 to 7 and 14 to 17) are typically considered to be process- or skill-oriented domains because they primarily represent *personal skills* effective principals are expected to use on the job. On the other hand, the remaining ten domains (8 to 13 and 18 to 21) are usually seen to be content-focused domains because they primarily represent *knowledge* that principals must have to develop specific decisions and effective courses of action.

While this distinction between skill-oriented and content-oriented domains has proven to be helpful in conceptualizing and assessing the performance of a principal, readers are encouraged to keep in mind that both knowledge and skill expectations are presented in each of the twenty-one domains. Accordingly, this theme is consistently emphasized in each of the books in the School Leadership Library.

In general, both practitioners and professors are in agreement with the expectations elaborated in *Principals for Our Changing Schools*; however, most have adopted the position that these expectations, taken collectively across the twenty-one domains, represent the *ideal school principal*. Thus, not every principal is expected to have the personal knowledge and skills required to meet all expectations put forth for each of the twenty-one domains.

With this ideal structure in the forefront, current thinking usually focuses on two realistic strategies.

First, both prospective and practicing school principals should be convinced to recognize that meeting expectations in these twenty-one domains is clearly essential for school principals to be effective on the job. Creating a professional advocacy for this position on effectiveness is seen by most active proponents to be the joint responsibility of school and university colleagues involved in the professional development of school principals.

How this joint responsibility might work is detailed in *Principals for the Schools of Texas: A Seamless Web of Professional Development*, a policy position paper written by Erlandson (1997) and published by the Sid W. Richardson Foundation.

Second, because school principals are not likely to have all of the knowledge and skills required to meet the ideal expectations specified in the NPBEA typology, they will need (at least in the short-run) to work collaboratively with other professionals in the school community who have the *balance of expertise* required to define and solve real-world problems of practice.

Those who support this strategy anticipate that school principals will view this collaborative problem-solving activity as an integral part of their continuing professional education. Accordingly, using shared expertise on the job to address the routine and emerging problems of practice is seen as a meaningful way for practicing school principals to extend and improve their current level of competence.

Two examples of how collaboration becomes an excellent strategy for continuing professional education on the job are the campus-based leadership laboratory described in Zellner and

Erlandson (1997) and the field-based action research strategy described in Scribner and Bredeson (1997).

This chapter focuses on the second strategy given above. It explores ways that the measurement and evaluation expertise of professional colleagues can be used by school principals in collaborative problem solving. Such expertise resides in many school and community professionals. Among these are counselors, nurses, school psychologists, program evaluation specialists, curriculum coordinators, and social workers.

While any one of these professional colleagues could be our focus, we have chosen to highlight how the professional expertise of school psychologists can be used in collaborative problem solving.

Focusing on the school psychologist has two primary advantages. First, it allows us to introduce a variety of school problems whose solutions typically involve the use of measurement and evaluation expertise. Second, this focus will alert school principals to the emerging interest among school psychologists to become more actively involved in school and classroom activities (see, for example, Talley, Kubiszyn, Brassard, and Short, 1996).

With these ideas in mind, this chapter provides answers to three specific questions.

- ◆ What is a school psychologist?
- ◆ How can school psychologists help principals solve routine and emerging problems they encounter in practice?
- ◆ What are the characteristics of successful collaboration?

Keeping the order given above, the balance of the chapter is divided into three parts, each part providing an answer to one question.

THE SCHOOL PSYCHOLOGIST

In *The Diploma in School Psychology*, the American Board of Professional Psychology (ABPP, 1997), a credentialing body for professional psychologists, notes that school psychology is the application of the science and profession of psychology to the questions and issues related to the protection and promotion of the academic and personal development of children and youth.

This ABPP publication suggests two primary functions that school psychologists perform. First, school psychologists facilitate the development of children and youth through learning activities in formal as well as informal educational settings. Second, school psychologists bring their expertise to bear on challenges that confront adults who, through their involvement in a variety of educational entities, are part of the schooling enterprise for children and youth.

In the *Handbook of School Psychology*, Bardon (1982) provides a similar description using a question-and-answer format. He suggests that if you ask school psychologists what they do, you are likely to receive a detailed list of the many functions they perform, including "virtually everything that can be done by professional psychologists of any kind or persuasion, but with emphasis on their performance in school or with school-age children and their families" (p. 3).

WHERE DO SCHOOL PSYCHOLOGISTS WORK?

School psychologists are found in a variety of settings, performing a variety of services. They not only work in public and private schools, but also in universities, clinics, institutions, private practices, community agencies and hospitals.

As in many other professions, such as engineering, law, medicine, and social work, school psychologists often work in two or more settings. For example, a school psychologist residing in a school district or a child clinic may also serve as an adjunct professor in a graduate school of education.

WHAT DO SCHOOL PSYCHOLOGISTS DO?

Bardon (1982) notes that school psychology evolved, in large part, from the interest in urban public schools in the 1930s to have more precise ways to identify and classify children for whom special school services were required.

While the basic reasons for having school psychologists have not changed over the years, most educators believe that the expanded services offered by today's school psychologists are the direct result of pressure from parents in local communities who have learned to appreciate the clinical services school psychologists can offer to improve the education and quality of life for children and their families.

A compilation of noteworthy clinical services appreciated by parents is given in *School Psychologists: Helping Educate All Children* published by the National Association of School Psychologists (1995). This compilation of over 200 examples coming from all 50 states, illustrates ways in which individual school psychologists have assisted in changing environments, attitudes, and systems to help children use their strengths to succeed in academic learning, social skills and citizenship. Following is a sample of these services:

- *Helping* children overcome impediments to learning;
- *Integrating* special and regular education;
- *Creating* parent support groups for elementary school students with below-average reading skills;
- *Helping* students to improve organizational skills;
- *Designing* early intervention programs for at-risk kindergarten students;
- *Conducting* adult-literacy training that enables parents to become partners in helping their children learn;
- *Sharing* effective teaching techniques with classroom teachers;
- *Helping* schools to become family friendly;
- *Coordinating* access to community health and social service agencies;
- *Operating* a family advocate program in the schools;
- *Building* more effective home-school partnerships;
- *Implementing* a conflict-resolution/peer-mediation program that reduces time spent on discipline;
- *Offering* social skills training for students with behavioral disorders;

- ◆ *Training* teachers and administrators to deal effectively with violent behavior;
- ◆ *Intervening* on many levels during crises.

This NASP compilation is designed to be a networking publication. Accordingly, each of the 200-plus illustrations provide the name, phone number, and address of the school psychologist who has volunteered to share an intervention.

ARE SCHOOL PSYCHOLOGISTS INTERESTED IN COLLABORATION?

In their response to this question, McNamara, Grossman, Lapierre, and Laija (1998) argue that school psychologists clearly wish to move *beyond* being recognized solely as the person providing individual test scores (assessments) for decision making in special education and *toward* becoming a team player in the design, implementation, and evaluation of promising educational reforms.

Advocates of this expanded role for school psychologists include Bradley-Johnson, Johnson, and Jacob-Timm (1995), who recently predicted that "school psychologists will have an increasingly important role in working with teachers and other professionals in designing effective interventions for improving learning and classroom behavior" (p. 191).

Their predictions include several relevant interventions such as working with individual classroom teachers who now need more help to manage inclusion policies that place all students in regular classrooms, modifying instructional computer programs that are not effective for certain students, and assuming a proactive role in program evaluation by introducing single-subject and group research designs that can help determine when changes are needed and how effective these changes are once they have been introduced.

PRINCIPALS AND SCHOOL PSYCHOLOGISTS

The second question reflects the primary theme developed in this chapter. It specifically asks: *How can school psychologists help principals solve routine and emerging problems they encounter in practice?*

The response is based on experience gained in a Fall 1996 interdisciplinary seminar conducted on a high school campus. This field-based seminar was conducted by the first author. There were nine seminar participants. Three members of the seminar group were practicing school principals in urban Texas school districts. Three other members were school psychologists. The remaining three members were measurement and statistics specialists who work on educational research and program evaluation projects.

The response to Question Two takes the form of five illustrations that reflect the types of current school problems this seminar group believes can be addressed at the campus level using the combined expertise of school principals and school psychologists. Illustrations were chosen to represent a wide array of actual opportunities for collaborative problem solving discussed in this fifteen-week seminar.

The first two illustrations are based on actual case studies reported in the school psychology literature. Both cases include a final section that provides evidence indicating the basis on which the collaborative effort was judged to be successful. The last three illustrations are hypothetical. Accordingly, they include proposed rather than actual solutions.

ILLUSTRATION ONE: LINKING SCHOOL PSYCHOLOGISTS WITH TEACHERS

The first illustration views a school principal as a person who is able to link school psychologists with individual classroom teachers who need help. This case study was constructed using information found in Ysseldyke et al. (1997). This student case study is just one of several entries in a *typical day* diary for a school psychologist working in the schools.

Other entries in this one-day diary include these activities: *helping* a teacher plan for two students with moderate disabilities who are fully included in the regular classroom; *checking* with a teacher about a student who has been crying in class and having difficulty with a parental separation; *consulting* with a parent concerned about her child's test score; *conducting* a small group session of an ongoing social skills group with boys in second grade who have been targeted as individuals who could benefit from learning anger and control techniques; and *meeting* with a foster parent and a child-protection worker for a boy, new to this school, to determine if his placement in a stable home environment has eliminated his previous behavioral problems.

PROBLEM. Following the suggestion of a social worker, a special education classroom teacher visits with the school principal about a disruptive student who has been diagnosed as having fetal alcohol syndrome (FAS). The classroom teacher has questions about how the student's behaviors are related to FAS and if some of the inappropriate behaviors could be decreased.

SOLUTION. The principal requests the assistance of a school psychologist residing in the district's central office. The school psychologist and the teacher meet and discuss what behaviors this child is displaying and what the teacher has tried previously. The school psychologist shares information with the teacher on FAS and how it may be related to the child's behaviors. After discussing their concerns together with the student's parents, they all agree that it would be helpful to have the school psychologist observe the student in the classroom. During the classroom observation, it becomes clear that the student's negative attention-seeking behaviors are quite extreme.

The school psychologist, parents, and teacher meet again to discuss the classroom observation. The school psychologist noticed that the child took great lengths to seek out the attention of his peers. Together, they designed an intervention in which the peers are used to reinforce the student's positive behaviors and ignore his negative behaviors (see Broussard and Northup, 1995 and 1997).

RESULTS. The school psychologist follows up with the teacher a few days after the initial implementation of the plan to work out any problems. During the next thirty days, the school psychologist returns periodically to the classroom to observe the results of this solution. Direct observations of the student's behavior in the classroom reveal a significant and continuous reduction of disruptive behaviors. These positive results are shared with the principal, social worker and student's parents.

ILLUSTRATION TWO: REDUCING VIOLENCE ON THE SCHOOL CAMPUS

The Annual National Gallup Poll of Public Education and similar needs assessments (polls) recently conducted in local school districts reveal that U.S. adults believe that one of the biggest problems that needs to be addressed in the public schools in their community is violence and gangs (Peterson, 1997). The second illustration references this concern and is based on a case study published in Snapp, Hickman, and Conoley (1990).

PROBLEM. A junior high school was serving a neighborhood that had been all white and that was gradually being integrated (see Snapp and Sikes, 1977). During this time, the school staff observed a dramatic increase in physical confrontations between students.

The school staff believed that a systematic group counseling program, focusing on counselor availability to intervene and to induce controlled verbal confrontations, would be a good way to avoid physical confrontations. Additional collaborative fact finding led the staff to recommend that a school psychologist was needed to train the counselors in small group techniques. Accordingly, the school principal and a counselor requested a conference with the school psychologist who was asked to assist in planning the group counseling program for this junior high school.

SOLUTION. The school psychologist observed that the school's faculty was very supportive of the proposed need for a group counseling program, especially because they were very concerned about the increase in fighting.

The school psychologist agreed to provide training in group skills for the counselors and the students and to co-lead a group for each counselor during the current school year. Specifically, the school psychologist's supervision would concentrate on using the group experiences as a means to focus on issues that group co-leaders could review after each session.

RESULTS. After the initial year of this group counseling program, an evaluation project was undertaken. In this evaluation, the actual number of fights was tabulated and analyzed. These evaluation results indicated that for the first time in four years there had not been an increase in the number of physical alterca-tions. Moreover, in comparison to the senior high school serving the same changing student populations, desegregation in this junior high school advanced more smoothly and with little difficulty.

LONG-TERM CONSEQUENCES. This group counseling pro-gram was continued for more than eight years. Almost all of the teachers on the junior high school staff were trained by the school psychologist during the first three years. Subsequent training was provided to new teacher volunteers by the counsel-ors themselves, with assistance from the school psychologist when needed. The program became a regular part of the overall school program.

In addition, this clearly defined junior high school strategy (implemented by committed school administrators, counselors, and teachers) became a manual for group counseling activities in the school district. The manual was also widely disseminated throughout the state, and it received state and federal commen-dations for its usefulness as a training guide. Principals inter-ested in experimenting with this strategy are encouraged to ex-amine the complete text and supporting evidence provided in Snapp, Hickman, and Conoley (1990).

ILLUSTRATION THREE: CONSTRUCTING PORTFOLIOS TO ASSESS STUDENT LEARNING

Interest in developing useful alternatives to standardized testing in the schools has proliferated in the past decade. For ex-ample, it is now common practice for many local, state, and na-tional professional associations to sponsor conferences to con-sider alternative ways to assess student performance. Interest has also extended to state legislatures, which are looking toward mandating the use of alternative assessments as a means to de-termine how well schools and school districts are performing.

In *Measurement and Evaluation in the Schools*, Worthen, Borg, and White (1993) note that several labels have been used to de-scribe alternative assessment, with the most common being di-rect assessment, authentic assessment, performance assessment and portfolio assessment. While there are subtle distinctions, these three authors believe that all alternative assessments share two commonalties: they are all viewed as alternatives to traditional multiple-choice tests; and they all refer to direct examination of student performance on significant tasks relevant to life outside the classroom.

This illustration deals with a genuine interest in developing a portfolio assessment strategy on an elementary school campus. It assumes portfolio assessment to be a collaborative assessment in that a well-defined portfolio assessment requires students and teachers to become partners in learning. Development of this illustration draws extensively from the excellent treatment of portfolio assessment given in Worthen, Borg, and White (1993, Chapter 15). Our seminar discussions of portfolio assessment were also informed by review of Birrell and Ross (1996), Cizek (1996), and Irwin-DeVitis (1996).

PROBLEM. At a campus faculty meeting a majority of classroom teachers share an interest in investigating portfolio assessment as a means to improve the measurement of student learning. To this point, the assessment of basic skills at this elementary school has been dominated by paper-and-pencil tests. At the close of the meeting, the school principal agrees to follow through on their interest.

SOLUTION. Additional conversations with the faculty, and with a school psychologist who has helped several classroom teachers on the campus, led the school principal to form an ad hoc planning group to work on the development of a portfolio assessment strategy.

The school principal designated this school psychologist and a classroom teacher who had experience with portfolio assessment to co-chair the campus planning group. Other members of the group would be volunteer teachers. The principal also volunteered to be a working member of the group.

As the commissioning agent, the school principal prepared a written charge for the planning group. This charge required the group to complete two specific phases of work and report the findings of each phase to the faculty.

The first phase was an information seeking phase where the group was asked to provide answers to these basic questions.

♦ What is a portfolio?

♦ What does a portfolio look like?

♦ What should a portfolio contain?

♦ Where should portfolios be kept?

The group was also encouraged to answer other questions that emerged as they worked toward the completion of the fact finding tasks outlined for phase one.

The second phase charged the planning group to develop a scope of work statement and schedule (time line), using as their guide the five basic steps given in Worthen, Borg, and White (1993, Chapter 15):

Step One.   Deciding what the portfolio should look like.

Step Two.   Deciding what goes into the portfolio.

Step Three. Deciding how and when to select portfolio samples.

Step Four.   Deciding how to evaluate portfolios.

Step Five.   Deciding what should be done with port-folios at the end of a school year.

At their first meeting the planning group decided it would complete both tasks in sixty days.

REFLECTIONS. The seminar group offered three reasons why the school psychologist would be an excellent choice to co-chair this elementary school planning group.

In general, school psychologists are more likely than class-room teachers or school principals to have direct experience in using assessments. Specifically, school psychologists have skills in reviewing multiple indicators of performance and combining these indicators to reach critical decisions regarding individual students.

School psychologists are more likely than teachers or ad-ministrators to be knowledgeable about reliability and validity issues that must be addressed in creating and using alternative assessments. This form of technical assistance was seen to be critical since portfolio assessment requires careful attention to be given to an array of measurement concerns, including content validity, generalizability across performance tasks and interrater reliability among judges of student portfolios.

School psychologists are trained and experienced in implementing group process strategies, including organizational development strategies that are designed to build group problem-solving capabilities (see McNamara, Dickson, and Guido-DiBrito (1988) and Schmuck (1990)).

The seminar group also believed that the principal's decision to have a classroom teacher co-chair this collaborative problem-solving group was an excellent decision because successful large-scale alternative assessments depend heavily on close linkage of assessment with actual classroom instruction.

ILLUSTRATION FOUR: EVALUATING AN INCLUSION POLICY AT THE CAMPUS LEVEL

Schools across the nation continue to reform their instructional programs in an attempt to provide the least restrictive environment for special education services mandated in 1975 by Public Law 94-142 (Education of the Handicapped Act) and updated in the 1990 and the 1997 Individuals with Disabilities Education Acts. This federal legislation requires that students with disabilities be educated (to the maximum extent possible) in regular (general) education classes. This mandated change has been labeled *inclusion* and has required substantial modifications in the delivery of education in all schools.

Inclusion requires detailed knowledge of the three pieces of legislation referenced above, as well as an awareness and understanding of the 1990 civil rights legislation that resulted in the Americans with Disabilities Act. Specific knowledge domains include the eligibility requirements for placement, the continuum of placement options, physical restructuring requirements to accommodate special students, and the policy processes used to guide how and when placement decisions are made.

Using the findings from recent educational change research, Powell and Hyle (1997) argue that school principals are the primary agents for change in the schools. Accordingly, they advocate that school principals should assume the major leadership role in meeting seven specific criteria essential for successful inclusion programs.

The seven essential criteria used in Powell and Hyle (1997) are: administrative support; special education personnel support; accepting classroom atmosphere; appropriate curriculum; effective general teaching skills; peer assistance; and disability-specific teaching skills.

Prior to developing the hypothetical case study offered below, the seminar devoted two three-hour sessions to discussing the three actual case studies given in Powell and Hyle (1997). Their case studies were very insightful, especially because they reflect clear and extensive descriptions of how each of three high school principals met the seven essential criteria associated with successful inclusion programs. Moreover, the evaluation findings in this article also provided detailed elaborations for campus problems to be solved in the immediate future.

The primary source Powell and Hyle use to support their position on the principal as the main agent (or blocker) of change in the schools is Fullan (with Stiegelbauer, 1991), who note that "The principal is the person most likely to be in a position to shape the organizational conditions necessary for change" (p. 76).

PROBLEM. Findings from a school district's strategic planning survey of parents, teachers and students indicated that one of the major problems to be addressed at each campus was the way the school district's new inclusion policy was being implemented.

At the administrative cabinet meeting following the release of the survey results, the superintendent charged each school principal to establish a campus committee to evaluate the procedures the faculty are currently using to implement the school district's new inclusion policy. The superintendent also noted that these evaluations were to be conducted with a view toward recommending ways each campus could improve their current inclusion program.

PROPOSAL. When the high school principal returned to the campus she decided to use the campus improvement committee already in place to conduct the evaluation study. She also asked a school psychologist, who was currently working with classroom teachers, to join the campus improvement committee.

At the first committee meeting, which was used to plan the evaluation, the school psychologist shared the seven criteria provided in Powell and Hyle (1997). The school psychologist also offered two suggestions that the committee agreed would help to focus the evaluation.

The first suggestion was that the committee should have, as soon as possible, a literature review indicating what inclusion strategies are likely to be most effective in high schools. The school psychologist offered to have an intern working with her prepare this review.

The second suggestion involved using the networking publication produced by the National Association of School Psychologists (1995). She told the committee that this publication contained a list of several school psychologists residing in eight different states who volunteered to share information about the successful inclusion programs currently operating in their school districts.

The school psychologist suggested that the high school principal join her to conduct telephone conference calls with these eight school psychologists. Her specific proposal suggested that, after each call, they should evaluate the shared information and, after all conference calls were completed, they should prepare a summary report for the committee, indicating the strategies they believed had promise at the high school.

REFLECTIONS. The seminar group decided that involving the school psychologist to help formalize the evaluation plan was an excellent idea. Two important reasons supporting this decision deserve mention.

First, school psychologists typically have a wide range of experience working with federal legislation that aims to create the least-restrictive environment for educating students with disabilities. This expertise can be used to assess both the legality and feasibility of suggestions proposed by the committee members.

Second, school psychologists are often familiar with and able to propose effective instructional and social interventions that can improve the implementation of an inclusion policy for all students. For example, their experience includes solutions for modifying instructional materials and equipment so that these resources work for all students. They are able to recommend practical strategies that reduce disruptive behavior and create a more accepting classroom atmosphere. School psychologists might also be instrumental in securing the support of special education personnel.

The seminar group also endorsed the idea that principals are (and can be) the primary agents for change in the schools. They noted that for classroom teachers, administrative support begins with the school principal.

A FOLLOW-UP ACTIVITY. Two principals in the seminar group declared an interest in learning more about adaptive technology. A school psychologist in the seminar offered to share some information on this topic in the next seminar session. A brief overview of the information shared on this topic is given below.

In general, over the past few years there has been a large-scale emphasis on incorporating computer technology into regular classroom instruction. Also of interest, many school psychologists have had excellent results in adapting computer technology for instructional use in special education classrooms. These efforts are frequently discussed in the professional education literature using terms such as *adaptive technology* and *assistive technology*.

Given these two general trends, school psychologists can be an excellent resource for using these assistive technologies in regular classrooms that are now operating under an inclusion policy.

ANOTHER FOLLOW-UP ACTIVITY. A year later, the same school psychologist mailed all seminar participants a copy of *Assistive Technology: A Handbook for Teachers,* which was an insert printed in the October 1997 issue of the monthly newsletter of the National Association of School Psychologists. This insert was published with the idea that it should be duplicated and shared in the schools.

The opening paragraph of this three-page insert reads: According to the Individuals with Disabilities Education Act (IDEA), an assistive technology is "any item, piece of equipment, or product system, whether acquired commercially off the shelf, modified, or customized, that is used to increase, maintain or improve functional capabilities of children with disabilities." The provision of assistive technology devices and services may be special education, related services or supplementary aids, and services to support a student with disabilities served in regular education (see 1997 Amendments to IDEA, Section 302).

It is of interest to note that each monthly issue of the National Association of School Psychology Newsletter includes an insert (practical information sheets) that school psychologists can share with principals and other professional colleagues.

ILLUSTRATION FIVE: PROVIDING RESEARCH AND EVALUATION ASSISTANCE TO SCHOOL PRINCIPALS

The final illustration moves from a specific to a general problem facing school principals. The illustration centers on the recognition that school principals are not always able to meet the ideal expectations put forth for all twenty-one domains specified in *Principals for Our Changing Schools*.

Examples of these ideal expectations from the measurement and evaluation domain are:

Applying different sampling methods to ensure objective, comprehensive, and effective assessment of student achievement;

Understanding why control is needed to increase the assurance that the measurement of student achievement is accurate;

Describing and reporting the uses and purposes of assessment, and the meaning and significance of essential assessment information to all who need to understand it;

Analyzing and interpreting many different sources of information appropriately, even when these sources may be inconsistent with each other;

Using knowledge of measurement error and statistical significance to interpret assessment results appropriately; and

Explaining the issues related to aggregation and disaggregation of assessment information, and when appropriate, to disaggregate information.

Ideal expectations from the information collection domain include these competencies:

Applying descriptive statistical analysis to summarize numerical test score information;

Calculating average scores for school-climate assessment;

Interpreting standard deviations for standardized test scores;

Applying graphics software applications to construct graphs and charts (this includes drawing bar graphs to highlight group differences and plotting test scores over time to illustrate trends);

Understanding procedures involved in collecting information through surveys, tests, interviews, observations, and document analysis; and

Evaluating information collection strategies against information needs and sources.

Examination of these two sets of requirements clearly suggests that effective school principals must have research expertise in areas such as sampling theory, experimental design, program evaluation, measurement theory, assessment techniques, survey research, statistical methods, document analysis, and computer graphics used in report preparation.

PROBLEM. Most school principals do not have formal training in the research areas elaborated above. Typically, a majority of their graduate training has been taken up by professional courses required for administrator certification. Until recently, few certification programs required enrollment in research courses, and certainly not at the technical level indicated above. Thus, there currently exists a gap between the ideal expectations given in *Principals for Our Changing Schools* and the actual competencies school principals have to meet these expectations.

Recognizing this gap, many informed school principals increase their effectiveness on the job by working collaboratively with other professionals in the school community who have the balance of research expertise needed to define and solve the real-world problems of practice.

PROPOSAL. The professional preparation of school psychologists, on the other hand, includes formal graduate level courses and practicum experience in research methods, measurement and statistics. This training puts school psychologists in an excellent position to be of direct assistance to school principals.

With this perspective in mind, school principals are encouraged to seek help from school psychologists on campus level projects that involve the use of research skills. Such projects include needs assessments, site-based management surveys, and evaluations undertaken with a clear intent to improve existing programs and services.

School psychologists should also be encouraged to share their research expertise with school principals. In addition to an invitation to work on campus research projects, school psychologists should consider volunteering their help to join ongoing or proposed collaborative research ventures.

REFLECTIONS. School principals in the seminar were quick to point out the continuing need for technical assistance in the interpretation of achievement test scores at the campus (aggregated) and classroom (disaggregated) levels. They frequently mentioned that many of their colleagues in the principalship experience constant pressure to increase achievement test scores on their campus. Most important, these same school principals indicated that they did not have the instructional design and measurement expertise needed to specify exactly what instructional objectives were directly responsible for poor test scores and, once these objectives were identified, how their classroom teachers might effectively adapt their current teaching practices to address these low performance areas.

In the seminar, this scenario was almost always linked directly to recent experiences principals had with their statewide achievement testing program and to the corresponding need for better alignment between their current curriculum guides and the instructional objectives contained in these mandated state level assessments.

Participants indicated that one of the most valuable *hands-on* activities in the seminar was the time devoted to an actual test alignment exercise conducted for a high school principal who shared her most recent statewide assessment results and the school district's curriculum guide used to focus mathematics instruction in ninth- through twelfth-grade classrooms. Results of this exercise pointed to specific classroom instructional areas where focused teaching should help to improve achievement scores in mathematics.

One seminar participant shared a school principal's interest in learning how an actual alternative assessment using student portfolios might be used as a means to improve performance on standardized achievement tests.

When seminar discussions first turned toward exploring how practicing school psychologists might assume a leadership role in research and evaluation, a member in the seminar shared a journal article describing the school psychologist as an action researcher.

This description (see Schmuck, 1990, p. 913) suggests that the school psychologist as action researcher "helps collect objective data—in the form of questionnaires, interviews, and observations—and then sees that the data are analyzed, discussed, and used for action planning." Focusing on intents and outcomes, the school psychologist as action researcher helps other research project collaborators "specify and clarify their shared problems, think of alternative actions to solve problems, use data in monitoring their success in implementing chosen actions, and use data to evaluate outcomes of their actions."

SUCCESSFUL COLLABORATION

While it has become commonplace in the educational literature to recommend collaboration, getting started on cooperative ventures requires answers to several key questions. How do people come together? Who provides the leadership for a collaborative? Who initiates and who responds? What problems can best be solved using collaborative strategies? How are collaborative action research projects identified? How are proposed new collaborative ventures approved?

Reflecting on her experience with these types of planning and organizational design questions, Lieberman (1985) suggested that the answers are not always as simple as they appear to be. More important, she has observed that the conventional wisdom about designing and operating collaborative efforts has given birth to a *mythology of collaboration* that has obscured and distorted the reality.

This situation led her to the position that the idea of collaboration and the experience of it are not the same. She illustrates this point in her insightful paper entitled *Enhancing School Improvement through Collaboration.*

MYTHS OF COLLABORATION

The Lieberman (1985) paper identifies four myths and then proposes some rules of thumb that can assist people who are dedicated to making collaboration work.

- ◆ *Myth One:* Collaboration must always begin with clear goals.

On the need for having precise goals before starting collaborative work, Lieberman suggests the following: "Somehow people get the idea that having clear goals will make the collaboration easier. But goals only become clear after people have worked together, taking some risks and acting upon their initial commitments to work together."

In a word, Lieberman believes that the goal statements written before a collaborative effort begins are no substitute for actually *experiencing* collaboration.

- ◆ *Myth Two:* Carefully planned activities are a necessity.

Like goals, planning in detail a set of specific activities seems to be the only rational thing to do. Lieberman suggests what is really needed are "one or two activities, flexibly planned with the idea that they can serve as a starting point for collaboration."

- ◆ *Myth Three:* There should be agreement made about definitions, major content, and structure before the collaborative agreement is endorsed.

Once again, this myth suggests that prespecified content and structure are always required for successful collaboration. On prespecification, Lieberman argues that this requirement also "ignores the time and experience it takes to learn to trust one another as well as to learn how to make collaboration work for mutual ends."

♦ *Myth Four:* A solid administrative structure and a permanent group of people are needed before any collaboration can take place.

Traditional leadership strategies almost always project leaders and followers operating in a familiar structure. Accordingly, we often overlook the idea of using some flexible arrangements involving people committed to working together *without* a single designated leader.

On this myth, Lieberman argues what is needed is "a core group of people who are willing and able to reach out to others, work with a variety of people and above all, create activities to make collaboration work."

GUIDELINES FOR SUCCESS

Lieberman (1985) believes that most successful collaborative ventures in the schools reflect strategies that defy traditional myths of large administrative structures, formal prespecified agreements, numerous planning and organizational design meetings, and clear goals before starting any collaborative work. Instead, productive collaborative efforts have:

♦ A firm commitment to collaborate;

♦ A small group of activists;

♦ Some small-scale beginning activities;

♦ A large measure of flexibility;

♦ A desire to learn from mistakes; and

♦ A great deal of comfort with ambiguity.

Seminar participants were in agreement with Lieberman's perspective on successful collaboration and indicated that this perspective has relevance for all five illustrations elaborated earlier in the second part of the chapter.

Seminar discussions on successful collaboration were informed by three additional review articles that dealt with changing schools from within (McNamara and McNamara, 1994), four perspectives on collaboration (McNamara, Wiseman, and McNamara, 1996), and myths to consider in planning and evaluating educational reforms (McNamara and McNamara, 1995b).

SUMMARY

The specific purpose of this chapter was to explore ways the professional expertise of school and community colleagues can be used by school principals in collaborative problem solving. While several professional colleagues could have been chosen to illustrate how principals can locate the balance of expertise required to define and solve real-world problems of practice, we elected to highlight how school psychologists can serve this role.

We saw two advantages in selecting school psychologists as our focus. This choice allowed us to introduce a variety of school problems whose solutions typically involve the use of measurement and evaluation expertise. This choice also allowed us to bring to the attention of school principals the emerging interest among school psychologists to become more actively involved in school and classroom activities.

Using three key questions, the chapter was divided into three parts, each providing an answer to one question.

The first part answered this question: *What is a school psychologist?* The answer to this question acknowledged that school psychologists are professionals trained specifically to work with preschoolers, children, adolescents, and their teachers and families. They also work with administrators and other school and community professionals to help make education for all students a positive and rewarding experience.

The second part shared five illustrations that reflect the type of current school problems an interdisciplinary graduate seminar group believed could be addressed at the campus level using the combined expertise of school principals and school psychologists.

The third part identified four myths of collaboration and, more importantly, specified some rules of thumb that can assist people who are dedicated to making collaboration work.

This perspective (Lieberman, 1985) suggested that most successful collaborative ventures reflect strategies that defy traditional myths of large administrative structures, formal prespecified agreements, numerous planning sessions, and clear goals. Instead, a productive collaborative venture should have a firm commitment to collaboration, a small group of activists, a few small-scale beginning activities, a large measure of flexibility, and a desire to learn from both successes and mistakes.

IMPLICATIONS

In developing answers to the three questions addressed in this chapter, three implications became evident.

First, this chapter represents just one example of how school principals can work collaboratively with other professionals in the school community who are likely to have the balance of expertise required to accurately define and solve the real-world problems of practice. Accordingly, school principals should also look toward other school professionals such as counselors, nurses, master teachers, program evaluation specialists, and social workers to join them on the job to address routine and emerging campus problems.

Second, if school psychologists wish to be influential members of school cultures (a position developed in Conoley and Gutkin, 1995), then they might give serious consideration to viewing school principals as a source of expertise to help them. Following this recommendation, there is clearly a companion position paper to be written. The title of this proposed companion position paper might be *The School Principal: A Source of Expertise Available to School Psychologists for Collaborative Problem Solving.*

Third, experience gained in the interdisciplinary graduate seminar referenced here lends additional support to the Tapasak and Keller (1995) recommendation that calls for having university-sponsored educational administration and school psychology courses that are co-taught and focused on collaborative problem-solving activities using integrated teams of teachers, administrators, school psychologists, and other professionals. In a word, if school principals and school psychologists are expected to work collaboratively, then it would appear that a simulation of this actual practicing professional environment in formal university courses and seminars would provide an excellent means to develop the necessary knowledge and skills for collaboration in the field.

Acknowledgments. The initial plans for this chapter profited from insights provided by three school principals, three school psychologists, and three measurement and statistics specialists who participated in a Fall 1996 interprofessional seminar on "Collaborative Problem Solving in Program Evaluation" conducted by the first author in the Bryan (Texas) Senior High School. Accordingly, we wish to thank Cynthia Barrett, Barry Grossman, Jason King, Wilda Laija, Coady Lapierre, Amy Minke, Karin Quenk, Deborah Sullivan, and Nilah Wright. Final plans for the design of this chapter were completed in an applied research project conducted in the first nine months of 1997 with the help of the three school psychologists who participated in the interprofessional seminar. We also wish to thank Jane Conoley, Jan Hasbrouck, and Jan Hughes, three professors from the Texas A&M University School Psychology Program, who contributed valuable research articles, professional reports, and suggestions used in this research project.

ACTION FOLLOW-UP

1. Identify a program evaluation project that can be conducted in a single elementary or secondary school. Outline a plan for conducting this program evaluation. Schedule a visit with a school counselor. Share your proposed plan and then ask the school counselor to evaluate your plan and to offer some suggestions for increasing the information value of the proposed evaluation for all stakeholders who have an interest in the program to be evaluated.

2. Using the same program evaluation outline, schedule a second visit with another professional colleague. Given the program you have chosen to evaluate, this colleague could be a curriculum specialist, school nurse, testing director, program evaluation specialist, social worker, or a central office administrator. Share your proposed plan and then ask this colleague to evaluate your plan and to offer some suggestions for improving your evaluation proposal. Identify the common and unique improvement strategies offered by the school counselor and the professional colleague you have chosen for the second visit.

3. Reread illustration four (p. 153) in this chapter. Schedule a visit with a school psychologist. Use the initial part of this visit to explain briefly the collaborative problem solving theme developed in this chapter. Next, ask the school psychologist to share an insert (practical information sheet) from one or more recent National Association of School Psychology (NASP) newsletters. If possible, use one of the inserts to explore ways you might collaborate to solve a relevant school problem.

7

MEASUREMENT AND EVALUATION ON THE JOB

The twenty-one books in the School Leadership Library were designed to show practicing and aspiring principals what they should know and be able to do to be effective leaders in the schools. These books apply the twenty-one domains of knowledge and skills recommended by the National Policy Board for Educational Administration (NPBEA). These domains are organized under four broad areas: Functional (seven domains), Programmatic (six domains), Interpersonal (four domains), and Contextual (four domains).

The twenty-one domains in this NPBEA classification (Thomson, 1993) are clearly not separate entities. They were developed with the idea that, taken collectively, they represent an efficient way to better understand the entire complex role of the school principal.

Because these domains are interactive rather than discrete, several books make direct reference to measurement and evaluation. For example, the importance of evaluation is emphasized in separate books in the series dedicated to domains such as problem solving, legal applications, organizational oversight, learning environments, and leadership. Similarly, the importance of these five domains was illustrated in earlier chapters in this book.

With these ideas in mind, this chapter references discussions of measurement and evaluation concerns in other books already published in the School Leadership Library. We believe that examining these references will contribute additional evidence to help readers better understand the importance of measurement and evaluation as a means to improve school leadership.

The specific focus in this chapter is on books already published in the first two broad areas. Accordingly, the chapter is divided into two parts. The first part provides connections between measurement and evaluation and the seven functional domains. The second part provides connections between measurement and evaluation and the other five programmatic domains.

FUNCTIONAL DOMAINS

The seven functional domains address the organizational processes and techniques by which the mission of the school is achieved. In more specific terms, these seven domains provide for the educational program to be realized and allow the school to function.

DOMAIN ONE: LEADERSHIP

In *Leadership: A Relevant and Realistic Role for Principals,* Crow, Matthews, and McCleary (1996) view leadership as an influence relationship. They believe principals exercise leadership both inside and outside the school by influencing others in the school community to join them in establishing an environment for school improvement. Moreover, they believe that the principal who is flexible and open to the potential leadership in others will be in a better position to influence relevant school improvement efforts.

We believe these three authors provide direct links between leadership and evaluation when they suggest that school principals exercise leadership by *encouraging* members of the school community to evaluate and revise mutual purposes for the school (p. 40), *performing* eight basic managerial tasks that influence goal accomplishment (p. 42), and *conducting* school efforts to evaluate the achievement of significant changes that represent the collective or pooled interest of the school community (p. 83).

Direct links are also provided when they suggest that principals exercise leadership by *communicating* the school's real achievements (i.e., evaluation results for effective and ineffective programs) to all stakeholders (p. 87) and *influencing* others to assess whether the school is successfully addressing its external and internal problems (p. 125).

The five page references inserted in the preceding paragraphs are for Crow, Matthews, and McCleary (1996). In each of the remaining domains discussed in this chapter, the parenthetical page references are to the relevant book in the School Leadership Library.

DOMAIN TWO: INFORMATION COLLECTION

In *Information Collection: The Key to Data-Based Decision Making*, Short, Short, and Brinson (1998) argue that school principals and their colleagues who share leadership roles in the schools must be able to use information to make critical decisions on important issues. They note that using an information approach will require school leaders to locate relevant data already available in the schools (archival data) and, in many cases, to collect additional data using valid and reliable measures.

Their approach also emphasizes a distinction we developed in Chapter 5 namely, *data* become *information* only when they are put into a form that speaks directly to the decision issues at hand.

In their book, one finds several examples that illustrate essential links between the information collection and the measurement and evaluation domains. Four excellent examples are *defining* program evaluation as organizational learning (p. 7); *describing* a needs assessment that uses survey questionnaires and a focus group session to generate information a school wanted to help improve the way it works with bilingual children and their families (p. 23); *elaborating* specific techniques that can be used to obtain evaluation data about school achievement (p. 48); and *illustrating* how an information source matrix can be constructed to guide an information analysis process in the schools related to at-risk students and academic failure (p. 82).

DOMAIN THREE: PROBLEM ANALYSIS

In *Problem Analysis: Responding to School Complexity*, Achilles, Reynolds, and Achilles (1997) indicate that the two main divisions of problem analysis are problem finding and problem solving. They believe that careful problem analysis is an essential precursor to educational improvement. Without a clear perspective on a problem and the ability to connect that problem to the purposes of education, they believe school leaders will quickly stray from the path to improving schools.

This book offers several opportunities to link problem analysis with the measurement and evaluation domain. Two specific examples are *declaring* the need for establishing rigorous evaluation designs to evaluate promising interventions implemented in the school (p. 23) and *illustrating*, in a case study about excessive discipline referrals, that administrative decisions based on evidence (data) should usually be preferred to decisions based solely on opinions (p. 41).

Three additional examples are *using* demographic data to create a scenario that defines problems to be addressed in program evaluation and strategic planning (p. 55); *introducing* validity and reliability as essential criteria for evaluating the credibility and accuracy of all information sources (p. 77); and *specifying* evaluation as the final step in the problem analysis cycle (p. 84).

DOMAIN FOUR: JUDGMENT

In *Judgment: Making the Right Calls*, Sweeney and Bourisaw (1997) argue that good judgment on the part of the principal is a fundamental requirement for support of an orderly learning process. They believe that good judgment involves reaching logical conclusions and making high quality, timely decisions based on the best available information. Moreover, they believe that making *good judgment calls* is the most important activity of the principalship.

Many of the suggestions Sweeney and Bourisaw offer for making good judgment calls can be linked directly to measurement and evaluation strategies. Two examples are *defining* problems as gaps between a desired state (what should be) and a current state (what actually is) (p. 12), and *distinguishing* between a mission statement and a problem so that a problem can be defined in terms that narrow its scope and provide sufficient specificity to be attainable and measurable (p. 13).

Additional links can be observed in their recommendations for data collection and analysis of data. Specifically, they emphasize the need for principals *to ask* themselves whether they have sufficient information to confidently answer important questions (p. 62), *to check* the reliability and expertise of those providing facts (p. 66), and *to determine* if facts are internally consistent or contradictory (p. 66).

When facts are contradictory or inconsistent, they recommend that the principal conduct follow-up activities to determine their validity or accuracy. Accordingly, they caution principals about being "in too much of a hurry to collect needed information" (p. 69). The importance of this caution was emphasized in our response to Question 18 (which is found on p. 113 of this book) where we indicated that credibility requires both prolonged engagement and persistent observation.

DOMAIN FIVE: ORGANIZATIONAL OVERSIGHT

In *Organizational Oversight: Planning and Scheduling for Effectiveness*, Erlandson, Stark, and Ward (1996) suggest that organizational oversight involves five specific functions. These are:

- *Planning and Scheduling* one's own and others' work so that resources are used appropriately and short- and long-term priorities and goals are met;
- *Scheduling* flows of activities;
- *Establishing* procedures to regulate activities;
- *Monitoring* projects to meet deadlines;
- *Empowering* the process in appropriate places.

They believe that when all stakeholders have an integral part in planning, scheduling, establishing and monitoring, they are empowered. Moreover, they believe that the principal's competence in the organizational oversight domain will directly affect how empowered stakeholders actually become.

Although it is not the primary focus of their book, Erlandson, Stark, and Ward acknowledge that program evaluation is an essential part of planning, and planning is at the heart of organizational oversight.

With this perspective in mind, they suggest (p. 4) that program evaluation is essentially an assessment by stakeholders using these five questions about school organization:

- What should the goals and objectives of the school be?
- What resources need to be applied to meet these objectives?
- How can these resources be most effectively and efficiently applied?
- How well have we met the school's goals and objectives?
- How can our answers to these questions guide our planning in the future?

They believe that all five of these evaluation questions are important at every level of planning. However, they indicate that greater emphasis is given to the first, fourth, and fifth questions in strategic planning, and to the second and third questions in short-range planning (p. 5).

DOMAIN SIX: IMPLEMENTATION

In *Implementation: Making Things Happen*, Pankake (1998) notes seven characteristics found repeatedly in successful implementation efforts: clear purposes and directions; continued advocacy; resource support; continued training and development; regular progress checks (formative evaluation); mechanisms to provide continuous feedback; and the common belief by implementors that the project or program is both useful to do and able to be done.

The importance of measurement and evaluation in implementation can be found in three themes that are well-developed in this book.

- Baseline Data

Pankake suggests that developing baseline data and comparison standards are essential requirements for evaluating progress toward a goal. Specifically, knowing where we started helps us to measure how we have progressed. Without a measure of where we started, we can only guess at how far we may have come. Thus, time spent developing descriptions of the current situation will prove its worth when we look toward evidence to determine if we are making progress (p. 32).

♦ Formative Evaluation

Pankake believes that principals can make implementation easier by providing continuous feedback that evaluates progress. By creating feedback loops for sharing formative evaluation data, principals facilitate positive attitudes and task completion. On the other hand, failure to share formative evaluation data can cause school colleagues to doubt the sincerity of those directing a program or project (p. 71).

♦ Archival Data

Principals and their colleagues in the schools responsible for monitoring the implementation of a program or project should recognize that a great deal of data useful in monitoring the program or project is already available in the schools.

On this point, Pankake notes that data of all kinds are collected daily, weekly, monthly, and annually. For example, data such as student attendance files, immunization records, standardized test scores, end-of-semester grades, staff attendance, and equipment and supply purchases are collected regularly in most schools. These data may be collected for reasons other than monitoring the implementation of a program, project or process in the school. However, if the data are determined to be directly related to the goals and objectives of the effort, they should be used for the purpose of monitoring and evaluation as well (p. 118).

DOMAIN SEVEN: DELEGATION

In *Delegation and Empowerment: Leading With and Through Others*, Ward and MacPhail-Wilcox (1998) argue that delegation is one dimension of democratic leadership. It includes distributing responsibility among members of the school organization, empowering these members, and aiding their participation in the decision-making process. They believe that a prudent school leader will recognize that delegation has tremendous potential to build leadership capacity in others, as well as enhance the achievement of important organizational goals and objectives.

Their position on the links between delegation and empowerment can be summarized as follows: When members of the school community are delegated a task with appropriate responsibility and resources with which to accomplish the task, they are empowered to contribute or develop their skill and knowledge toward the accomplishment of something important to the welfare of students, teachers, parents, and the school community.

From an evaluation and planning perspective, they note, in Chapter 2, that the most commonly recommended systemic strategy for empowering school professionals and communities is a team-oriented performance strategy called site-based management. Using this strategy, a school community can become a dynamic learning unit dedicated to collectively searching for performance problems (problem defining) and to jointly implementing improvements that can be evaluated for effect (problem solving).

In the final chapter of their book, the authors summarize the ways a school principal can become proficient in the delegation and empowerment process. Their summary provides an excellent overview of specific skills described in earlier chapters.

Their summary concludes by noting that it seems self-evident that school leaders will be interested in the quality of results obtained when decisions and tasks are delegated. In spite of this, the authors observe that systematic evaluation and follow up rarely occur in any formal manner. While they agree that exhaustive evaluations and follow-up activities may be impractical, they recommend that it is useful to evaluate the process and results of delegation. They believe that this formal evaluation can provide insights into the degree of success realized and guide future related tasks.

PROGRAMMATIC DOMAINS

While the seven functional domains are typically considered to be process- or skill-oriented domains because they primarily represent *personal skills* that effective principals use on the job, the six programmatic domains are usually seen as content-focused domains because they primarily represent *knowledge* that principals must have to develop specific decisions and effective courses of action.

In the NPBEA classification, the six programmatic domains focus specifically on the scope and framework of the educational program. They reflect both the core technology of schools, which is instruction, and the related school services, developmental activities, and resource base that are needed to support instruction.

DOMAIN EIGHT: INSTRUCTION AND LEARNING ENVIRONMENT

In *Instruction and the Learning Environment*, Keefe and Jenkins (1997) indicate that the effective principal for today's school must have a strong foundation for demonstrating instructional leadership.

Keefe and Jenkins believe that this foundation requires a principal to recognize the need *for conceptualizing* the school as a learning organization; *for understanding* the role of information processing, instructional models, learning styles and student motivation in creating productive learning environments; and *for understanding* how new forms of authentic assessment and action research can be used to extend the constant search for better ways to teach and learn in the schools.

The importance of measurement and evaluation in the instruction and learning environment domain is clearly evident in two concepts developed in separate chapters in this book.

AUTHENTIC ASSESSMENT. If students are to prize high quality intellectual work, Keefe and Jenkins (Chapter 4) argue, then assessment tasks must signal that knowledge construction (not merely recall), disciplined inquiry, and real-world products are highly valued.

Using these three characteristics, Keefe and Jenkins elaborate seven standards principals and teachers can use to evaluate the merit and worth of a proposed authentic assessment task. Their elaboration is summarized below.

An authentic assessment task that calls for the *construction of knowledge* must require a student (1) to organize information in a systematic way and (2) to consider alternatives that reflect differing perspectives, strategies, and solutions (p. 61).

An authentic assessment task that reflects *disciplined inquiry* must require a student (3) to demonstrate an understanding of disciplinary content (subject matter), (4) to use appropriate methods of inquiry for the discipline, and (5) to provide an elaborated written communication that exhibits one's understandings, explanations, findings and conclusions (p. 62).

An authentic assessment task that reflects *value beyond the classroom* must require students (6) to select a problem addressing a real-world issue and (7) to communicate their knowledge, design a product, present a performance, or take an action that relates to a real-world audience (p. 64).

ACTION RESEARCH. While all research involves systematically accumulating and interpreting evidence, Keefe and Jenkins (1997, Chapter 9) suggest that action research focuses on evidence that helps school practitioners to determine whether their own actions help students reach desirable ends. Action research is often called practitioner or teacher research because it places the control of school improvement in the hands of teachers, groups of teachers and building-level administrators.

Action research has many forms. It can be conducted by an individual teacher, a group of teachers or a principal. An alternate action research design might involve an entire professional team gathering data to determine the relative effectiveness of a specific school-level innovation (p. 163).

Action research and evaluation share a common purpose and use the same inquiry methods. Accordingly, action research can be used by a principal as an integral part of a school-level evaluation project.

Integrated in this manner, action research can give a school evaluation project a distinct advantage because it operates on this positive assumption put forth by Keefe and Jenkins: the more that recommendations for school improvement are derived from the setting in which they are to be implemented, the higher the degree of commitment on the part of the staff (p. 160).

DOMAIN NINE: CURRICULUM DESIGN

At this time the book on the curriculum design domain has been commissioned, but has not yet been published. Thus, we are unable to reference it here. However, we will reference one noteworthy source that illustrates the connection between the curriculum and the measurement and evaluation domains.

In *Measurement and Evaluation in the Schools*, Worthen, Borg, and White (1993) note that many schools and school districts have developed long-range curriculum evaluation plans that are cyclical, with periodic reviews scheduled in a staggered fashion. Accordingly, some curriculum areas are evaluated each year and every curriculum area is evaluated at a reasonable interval.

Principals interested in long-range, cyclical curriculum evaluation in their schools are encouraged to set the time interval at five years, a time frame frequently used in strategic planning.

DOMAIN TEN: STUDENT GUIDANCE AND DEVELOPMENT

In *Student Guidance and Development*, Ward and Worsham (1998) provide principals and their professional colleagues with user-friendly ideas and strategies related to meeting the developmental needs of students in the schools. They review many successful programs that have been put in place at schools across the country.

While their emphasis is not on theory, but is instead on practical suggestions, the authors devote their first chapter to introducing some of the theories developed by prominent thinkers regarding how children develop. On the importance of this knowledge they suggest that "revisiting Child Development 101 from time to time helps both administrators and teachers look for solutions based on the emotional, social, and physical needs of students" (p. 2).

Ward and Worsham believe that an effective principal needs to be an advocate for using site-based management teams to evaluate all school programs and services designed to meet the individual academic, social, and behavioral needs of students.

Advocacy on the part of the principal can be demonstrated by sharing essential criteria (knowledge) needed to define and measure concepts included in a school mission statement. For example, they identify fourteen positive outcomes (measurement domains) that a principal can share with a site-based management team commissioned to evaluate the concept of a school as a learning community (p. 35).

Advocacy can also be demonstrated by a principal who forms a site-based management team to collect teacher, parent and student survey data that will help the school community to have a better understanding of how to meet students' social as well as academic needs (pp. 30 and 65).

DOMAIN ELEVEN: STAFF DEVELOPMENT

In *Staff Development: Practices That Promote Leadership in Learning Communities*, Zepeda (1999) views staff development as an integral part of organizational learning. Its specific purpose is to improve the professional performance of school staff members.

Staff development efforts at the school level include programs for *improving* an existing practice, *implementing* a new program or service, *introducing* new curriculum objectives and *inducting* new faculty members. A well-designed and implemented staff development program is the important link that connects faculty and staff to their school and results in the improvement of instruction.

If personal and professional growth is to be maintained in the schools, Zepeda believes that principals must be directly and consistently involved in staff development. Through this involvement they can create positive and productive school cultures.

Searching for connections between the staff development and the measurement and evaluation domains is an easy task because Chapter 7 in Zepeda's book is devoted explicitly to identifying the basic components of program evaluation and elaborating their implications for principals as evaluators of staff development. Two themes developed in the chapter are especially helpful for understanding the connections between these two domains.

PRINCIPAL AS A ROLE MODEL. As with any other phase of staff development, Zepeda argues that the most effective way for principals to show leadership in evaluation is through modeling. Specifically, when classroom teachers see principals evaluating their own learning, as well as participating in the evaluation of the school's learning, they are much more likely to be active in evaluation themselves.

REPORTING EVALUATION RESULTS. When principals model the evaluation process, they are expected to communicate evaluation results to decision makers in a written report.

Zepeda suggests these seven concerns be used to organize the report:

♦ Goals that were established and why;

♦ Activities implemented to meet the goals;

♦ Persons who participated;

♦ Resources used;

♦ Satisfaction of participants;

♦ Impact on participants, specific programs and the institutions; and

♦ Recommendations for changes in the program.

Evaluation reports are often shared in a formal reporting session open to all stakeholders. In this situation, Zepeda suggests that the principal and other school leaders designated to collaborate in the presentation, should try to anticipate what questions the audience wants addressed. For example, school board trustees may have different concerns than the parent-teacher organization.

In best practice, anticipation begins in the design of the evaluation and remains a central concern all the way through to planning the preparation of the final report. To ensure that a written report and, when appropriate, the formal presentation of results are responsive, Zepeda recommends that a draft of the final report be circulated to key stakeholders for their comments.

DOMAIN THIRTEEN: RESOURCE ALLOCATION

In *Resource Allocation: Managing Money and People*, Norton and Kelly (1997) argue that today's school leaders must recognize the importance of achieving the maximum benefit from the resources received and used by the schools. This challenge continues to reinforce the need for school leaders to understand both the economics of school finance and what is required in human resource planning to create an equitable allocation of resources that effectively serve all students.

In every chapter of their book, one finds several concrete examples of how resource allocation is dependent on using evaluation information to guide decision making.

In Chapter 2, Norton and Kelly indicate that a needs assessment is the first step in making intelligent budget decisions. Needs assessment information permits the principal and the school planning team to gain perspectives on conditions at the school, student performance, and stakeholder perceptions. These perspectives are used to generate a school improvement plan that guides budget negotiations about the allocation of available funds.

In Chapter 3, Norton and Kelly identify procedures for gathering evidence to evaluate the actual utilization of financial resources. Here they describe the Goal Achievement/Resource Allocation Worksheet that provides the principal and the school planning team with a clear and succinct summary of fund allocations, goal achievement, and team conclusions and recommendations.

In Chapter 4, Norton and Kelly outline a data-based approach to evaluate the allocation of human resources used in staffing, recruitment, and personnel selection. They show how one can organize and analyze data from several sources, including credentials from the placement office, personal interview data, on-site teacher observations, videotapes of teacher performance, and other evidence reflecting creative talents.

In Chapter 5, Norton and Kelly specify data-based strategies to evaluate school climate, the instructional responsibilities of individual teachers, and staff development.

The importance of administrative responsibility in resource allocation is a continued theme emphasized in each of these four chapters. Also emphasized throughout their book, using a variety of summary worksheets, is the theme that *data* become *infor-*

mation only when data are put into a form that speaks directly to the decision issues at hand.

SUMMARY

This chapter located and shared discussions of measurement and evaluation concerns in twelve other books already published in the School Leadership Library. Seven of these books addressed functional domains representing personal skills effective principals use on the job and an additional five books addressed programmatic domains representing knowledge principals must have to develop specific decisions and effective courses of action.

The results of this search and the summary of findings reported in this chapter add additional evidence to support the idea that the twenty-one domains in the original NPBEA classification are not separate entities but rather represent an efficient way to better understand the entire complex role of the school principal.

The results of this search also support the idea that effective principals exercise leadership both inside and outside the school by influencing others in the school community to join them in establishing an environment for school improvement. Using this collaborative approach, a school community becomes a dynamic learning organization dedicated to collectively searching for performance problems and committed to cooperatively implementing improvements that can be evaluated for effect.

APPENDIX

SELF-APPRAISAL SYSTEM FOR MEASUREMENT

MEASUREMENT CONCEPTS (*see p. 86*)

Question 1. What is measurement? (*see p. 86*)

Question 2. What are the four most widely used measures in educational research and evaluation projects? (*see p. 87*)

Question 3. Behavioral science researchers frequently make a distinction between measurement and archival data. What is implied in this distinction? (*see p. 88*)

Question 4. The domain of interest in this text is *measurement and evaluation*. Although it is heuristic to combine these two terms to describe a single domain, there is a clear distinction between measurement and evaluation. What is this distinction? (*see p. 89*)

Question 5. In practice and professional study we often encounter the combined term *educational tests and measurements*. While these terms represent a single domain of interest to educators, there is a basic distinction between tests and measurements. What is this distinction? (*see p. 89*)

USES OF EDUCATIONAL MEASURES (*see p. 90*)

Question 6. When they are properly designed and appropriately applied by qualified professionals, tests yield results that can be used by a wide range of people. In general terms, who are some of the stakeholder groups (interested parties) likely to use test results? (*see p. 90*)

Question 7. How might each stakeholder group identified in the previous question use test results? (*see p. 91*)

Question 8. While there is clearly a wide range of reasons why stakeholders use test results, educational researchers have suggested that these reasons can be placed into a few general categories based on the types of decisions that are made using test results. What are these basic types of decisions? (*see p. 92*)

Question 9. What are some of the recent developments and trends in educational measurement that provide the current context for measurement and evaluation in the schools? (*see p. 94*)

Question 10. What is minimum competency testing? (*see p. 96*)

Question 11. What are the characteristics of minimum competency testing that will withstand legal challenges? (*see p. 97*)

Question 12. A key legal issue in the use of tests and other educational measures in schools is the right to privacy. What guidelines should principals establish in their schools to ensure that privacy rights and confidentiality are protected? (*see p. 98*)

Question 13. What ethical considerations should govern the use of tests in the schools? (*see p. 99*)

CONSTRUCTING NEW MEASURES (*see p. 104*)

Question 14. In quantitative inquiries, two essential characteristics for constructing new measures are validity and reliability. What is the distinction between these two essential characteristics? (*see p. 105*)

Question 15. Three common measurement procedures used to ensure confidence in the validity of a new quantitative measure are *content validity, concurrent validity,* and *predictive validity.* How would you describe these three measurement procedures and how might they be used in the schools? (*see p. 106*)

Question 16. Three common measurement procedures used to ensure confidence in the reliability of a new quantitative measure are *split-half reliability, parallel-form reliability,* and *test-retest reliability.* How would you describe these three measurement procedures and how might they be used in the schools? (*see p. 108*)

Question 17. In qualitative inquiries, two essential characteristics for constructing and interpreting new measures are *credibility* and *dependability.* What is the distinction between these two essential characteristics? (*see p. 111*)

Question 18. *Prolonged engagement, persistent observation, triangulation, referential adequacy materials, peer debriefing* and *member checks* are six strategies used to ensure credibility in qualitative inquiries. How would you describe these six strategies? (*see p. 113*)

Question 19. Creating an audit trail and using a reflexive journal are two strategies used to ensure dependability in qualitative inquiries. How would you describe these two strategies? (*see p. 114*)

CLASSIFYING MEASUREMENT
INSTRUMENTS (*see p. 116*)

Question 20. In your own words, describe and classify the measurement instruments that you have encountered in your professional work? (*see p. 116*)

Question 21. What are alternative assessments? (*see p. 120*)

INTERVIEWS AND DIRECT
OBSERVATION (*see p. 121*)

Question 22. A principal in your school district asks you to evaluate an action research project that was just completed in her school. This inquiry used interviews to collect all relevant data. What general guidelines would you specify to help you evaluate this campus research project? (*see p. 122*)

Question 23. A principal in your school district asks you to evaluate a standardized direct observation checklist that the campus committee has developed to gather classroom data for planning staff development activities dealing with effective teaching and student learning. What general guidelines would you identify to help you evaluate this school research project? (*see p. 124*)

QUESTIONNAIRE DESIGN
AND USE (*see p. 127*)

Question 24. You have just accepted the invitation to serve as a member of a school district's strategic planning committee that is now designing a needs assessment survey to guide the development of a new five-year plan. At the start of a survey planning session, each member of the committee is asked to construct one open-end and one closed-end questionnaire item. What is your response to this request? (*see p. 128*)

Question 25. What are the advantages and disadvantages of using open-end questions? (*see p. 130*)

Question 26. What are the advantages and disadvantages of using closed-end questions? (*see p. 131*)

Question 27. Your strategic planning committee is now ready to prepare the final report on the findings of its needs assessment survey. You are asked to provide some guidelines for publishing an accurate disclosure of the research design characteristics used in the survey. How would you respond? (*see p. 132*)

ADMINISTRATIVE DECISION MAKING (*see p. 134*)

Question 28. How would you define administrative decision making? (*see p. 134*)

Question 29. Decision theorists frequently make a distinction between data and information. What is implied in this distinction? (*see p. 135*)

Question 30. You are the principal on a campus that has a school-improvement committee. This committee asks you to provide some guidelines for planning the evaluation of a new instructional program that has operated in the school for the past two years. Assume that you are familiar with the importance of the distinction between data and information. How would you respond to their request? (*see p. 136*)

REFERENCES

■A■

Achilles, C.M., J.S. Reynolds, and S.H. Achilles. (1997). *Problem analysis: Responding to school complexity.* Larchmont, New York: Eye On Education.

Airasian, P.W. (1996). *Assessment in the classroom.* New York: McGraw-Hill.

Alkin, M.C., ed. (1992). *Encyclopedia of educational research.* 6th ed. New York: Macmillan.

American Board of Professional Psychology. (1997). *The diploma in school psychology.* Columbus, Mo.: American Board of Professional Psychology.

American Educational Research Association. (1985). *Standards for educational and psychological testing.* Washington, D.C.: American Educational Research Association.

■B■

Babbie, E. (1990). *Survey research methods.* 2d ed. Belmont, Calif.: Wadsworth.

Bardon, J.I. (1982). The role of the school psychologist: Opinion one. In *The handbook of school psychology,* edited by C.R. Reynolds and T.B. Gutkin. New York: John A. Wiley & Sons.

Birrell, J.R. and S.K. Ross. (1996). Standardized testing and portfolio assessment: Rethinking the debate. *Reading Research and Instruction* 35 (4): 285–97.

Borg, W.A., J.P. Gall, and M.D. Gall. (1993). *Applying educational research: A practical guide.* 3rd ed. White Plains, New York: Longman.

Bradburn, N.M. and S. Sudman. (1988). *Polls and surveys: Understanding what they tell us.* San Francisco, Calif.: Jossey-Bass.

Bradley-Johnson, S.C., M. Johnson, and S. Jacob-Timm. (1995). Where will —and where should—changes in education leave school psychology? *Journal of School Psychology* 33 (2): 187–200.

Broussard, C. and J. Northup. (1995). An Approach to functional assessment and analysis of disruptive behavior in regular education classrooms. *School Psychology Quarterly* 10 (2): 151–64.

———. (1997). The use of functional analysis to develop peer interventions for disruptive classroom behavior. *School Psychology Quarterly* 12 (1): 65–76.

■ C ■

Cizek, G.J. (1996). Grades: The final frontier in assessment reform. *NASSP Bulletin* 80 (576): 103–110.

Conoley, J.C. and T.B. Gutkin. (1995). Why didn't—why doesn't— school psychology realize its promise? *Journal of School Psychology* 33 (2): 209–19.

Cox, J. (1996). *Your opinion, please! How to build the best questionnaires in the field of education.* Thousand Oaks, Calif.: Corwin Press.

Crow, G.M., L.J. Matthews, and L.E. McCleary. (1996). *Leadership: A relevant and realistic goal for principals.* Larchmont, New York: Eye On Education.

■ D, E ■

Dillman, D.A. (1978). *Mail and telephone surveys: The total design method.* New York: John Wiley & Sons.

Dillman, D.A. and P. Salant. (1994). *How to conduct your own survey.* New York: John Wiley & Sons.

Eisenhart, M. and H. Borko. (1993). *Designing classroom research: Themes, issues, and struggles.* Boston, Mass.: Allyn and Bacon.

Erlandson, D.A. (1997). *Principals for the schools of Texas: A seamless web of professional development.* Fort Worth, Tex.: Sid W. Richardson Foundation.

Erlandson, D.A., E.L. Harris, B.L. Skipper, and S.D. Allen. (1993). *Doing naturalistic inquiry: A guide to methods*. Newbury Park, Calif.: Sage Publications.

Erlandson, D.A., P.L. Stark, and S.M. Ward. (1996). *Organizational oversight: Planning and scheduling for effectiveness*. Larchmont, New York: Eye on Education.

▪ F, G, H ▪

Fullan, M. (with S. Stiegelbauer). (1997). *The new meaning of educational change*. New York: Teachers College Press.

Gall, M.D., W.A. Borg, and J.P. Gall. (1996). *Educational research: An introduction*. 6th ed. White Plains, New York: Longman.

Gallagher, J.D. (1998). *Classroom assessment for teachers*. Upper Saddle River, N.J.: Merrill.

Gallagher, J.J. (1967). Teacher variation in concept presentation in BSCS curriculum programs. *BSCS Newsletter* 30: 8–19.

Gronlund, N.E. (1998). *Classroom assessment for teachers*. 6th ed. Boston, Mass.: Allyn and Bacon.

Gronlund, N.E. and R.L. Linn. (1990). *Measurement and evaluation in teaching*. 6th ed. New York: Macmillan.

Guba, E.G. and Y.S. Lincoln. (1981). *Effective evaluation*. San Francisco: Jossey-Bass, Publishers.

———. (1989). *Fourth generation evaluation*. Newbury Park, Calif.: Sage Publications.

▪ I, J ▪

Irwin-DeVitis, L. (1996). Teachers' voices: Literacy portfolios in the classroom and beyond. *Reading Research and Instruction* 35 (3): 223–36.

Jaeger, R.M. (1992). Competency testing. In *Encyclopedia of Educational Research*, edited by M.A. Alkin. New York: Macmillan.

Johnson, B. (1996a). *The performance assessment handbook: Portfolios and socratic seminars: Designs from the field and guidelines for the territory ahead*. Vol. 1. Larchmont, N.Y.: Eye On Education.

Johnson, B. (1996b). *The performance assessment handbook: Performances and exhibitions: Designs from the field and guidelines for the territory ahead.* Vol. 2. Larchmont, N.Y.: Eye On Education.

Joint Committee on Standards for Educational Evaluation. (1988). *The personnel evaluation standards.* Newbury Park, Calif.: Sage Publications.

————. (1994). *The program evaluation standards.* 2d ed. Thousand Oaks, Calif.: Sage Publications.

▪ K, L ▪

Keefe, J.W. and J.M. Jenkins. (1997). *Instruction and the learning environment.* Larchmont, New York: Eye On Education.

Leary, M.R. (1995). *Introduction to behavioral research methods.* 2d ed. Pacific Grove, Calif.: Brooks/Cole.

Lieberman, A. (1985). Enhancing school improvement through collaboration. In *Strengthening the role of the university in school improvement: Proceedings of the Allerton Symposium on Illinois Education Improvement.* University of Illinois, College of Education, Urbana-Champaign, Ill..

Lincoln, Y.S. and E.G. Guba. (1985). *Naturalistic inquiry.* Beverly Hills, Calif.: Sage Publications.

Linn, R.L. (1992). Achievement testing. In *Encyclopedia of educational research,* edited by M.A. Alkin. New York: Macmillan.

▪ M ▪

Madaus, G.F., ed. (1983). *The Courts, validity, and minimum competency testing.* Boston, Mass.: Kluever-Nijhoff.

McMillan, J.M. and S. Schumacher. (1993). *Research in education: A conceptual introduction.* 3rd ed. New York: Harper Collins.

McNamara, J.F. (1993). Administrative decision making: Part one. *International Journal of Educational Reform* 2 (4): 465–74.

————. (1994a). Administrative decision making: Part two. *International Journal of Educational Reform* 3 (1): 113–21.

———. (1994b). *Surveys and experiments in education research.* Lancaster, Pa.: Technomic Publishing Co.

———. (1997a). Parental views on the biggest problems facing public schools: National versus local findings. *International Journal of Educational Reform* 6 (3): 377–89.

———. (1997b). Questionnaire design for strategic planning. *International Journal of Educational Reform* 6 (1): 105–25.

———. (1998). Constructing a fact sheet: The first step in planning a meaningful survey. *International Journal of Educational Reform* 7 (2): 195–206.

McNamara, J.F. and M. McNamara. (1994). Two perspectives on change within schools. *International Journal of Educational Reform* 3 (2): 248–50.

———. (1995a). Collecting and analyzing decision-oriented data. In *Public relations in educational organizations: Practice in an age of information and reform,* edited by T.J. Kowalski. Englewood Cliffs, N.J.: Prentice Hall.

———. (1995b). Myths to consider when planning and evaluating educational reforms. *International Journal of Educational Reform* 4 (1): 120–22.

McNamara, J.F., M.A. Dickson, and F. Guido-Dibrito. (1988). Decision science perspectives for information systems and data administration. In *Handbook of information resource management,* edited by J. Rabin and E.M. Jackowski. New York: Marcel Dekker.

McNamara, J.F., B.G. Grossman, C.B. Lapierre, and W. Laija. (1998). The school psychologist: A source of expertise available to school principals for collaborative problem solving. *International Journal of Educational Reform* 7 (1): 80–94.

McNamara, M., D.L. Wiseman, and J.F. McNamara. (1996). Four perspectives on collaboration. *International Journal of Educational Reform* 5 (1): 128–32.

▪ N, O, P, Q ▪

National Association of School Psychologists. (1995). *School psychologists: Helping educate all children.* Bethesda, Md.: National Association of School Psychologists.

Norton, S.M. and L.K. Kelly. (1997). *Resource allocation: Managing money and people.* Larchmont, New York: Eye On Education.

Oosterhof, A. (1990). *Classroom applications of educational measurement.* Columbus, Ohio: Merrill.

Pankake, A.M. (1998). *Implementation: Making things happen.* Larchmont, New York: Eye On Education.

Peterson, G.J. (1997). Looking at the big picture: School administrators and school violence. *Journal of School Leadership* 7 (5): 456–79.

Powell, D. and A.E. Hyle. (1997). Principals and school reform: Barriers to inclusion in three secondary schools. *Journal of School Leadership* 7 (3): 301–26.

■ R, S ■

Sanders, J.R. (1994). The process of developing national standards that meet ANSI guidelines. *The Journal of Experimental Education* 63 (1): 5–12.

Sax, G. (1989). *Principles of educational and psychological measurement and evaluation.* 3rd ed. Belmont, Calif.: Wadsworth.

Schmuck, R. (1990). Organization development in schools: Contemporary concepts and practices. In *The handbook of school psychology,* edited by C.R. Reynolds and T.B. Gutkin. New York: John A. Wiley & Sons.

Scribner, J.P. and P.V. Bredeson. (1997). Beyond simulation and case studies: Improving leader preparation through action research. *Journal of School Leadership* 7 (3): 230–45.

Scriven, M. (1967). In *Curriculum evaluation,* edited by R.E. Stake. American Educational Research Association Monograph Series on Evaluation No. 1. Chicago: Rand McNally.

———. (1974). Standards for the evaluation of educational programs and products. In *Evaluating educational programs and products,* edited by G.D. Borch. Englewood Cliffs, N.J.: Educational Technology Publications.

———. (1991). *Evaluation thesaurus.* 4th ed. Newbury Park, Calif.: Sage Publications.

Short, P.M., R.J. Short, and K. Brinson. (1998). *Information collection: The key to data-based decision making.* Larchmont, New York: Eye On Education.

Simon, H.A. (1977). *The new science of management decision.* Rev. ed. Englewood Cliffs, N.J.: Prentice Hall.

Smith, E.R. and R.W. Tyler. (1942). *Appraising and recording student progress.* New York: Harper & Row.

Snapp, M. and J.N. Sikes. (1977). Preventive counseling for teachers and students. In *School consultation,* edited by J. Meyers, R. Martin, and I. Hyman. Springfield, Ill.: Charles C. Thomas.

Snapp, M., A.J. Hickman, and J.C. Conoley. (1990). Systems interventions in school settings. In *The handbook of school psychology,* edited by C.R. Reynolds and T.B. Gutkin. New York: John A. Wiley & Sons.

Stake, R.E. (1967). The countenance of educational evaluation. *Teachers College Record* 68: 523–40.

———. (1975). Program evaluation, particularly responsive evaluation. Occasional Paper No. 5. Kalamazoo, MI: Western Michigan University Evaluation Center.

———. (1978). The case study method in social inquiry. *Educational Researcher* 7: 5–8.

Stiggins, R.J. (1997). *Student-centered classroom assessment.* 2d ed. Upper Saddle River, N.J.: Merrill.

Stufflebeam, D.L., W.J. Foley, W.J. Gephart, E.G. Guba, R.L. Hammond, H.O. Merriman, and M.M. Provus. (1971). *Educational evaluation and decision making.* Itasca, Ill.: F.E. Peacock Publishers.

Sweeney, J. and D. Bourisaw. (1997). *Judgment: Making the right calls.* Larchmont, New York: Eye On Education.

■ T, U, V ■

Talley, R.C., T. Kubiszyn, M. Brassard, and R.J. Short. (1996). Making psychologists in schools indispensable: Critical questions and emerging perspectives. In *Proceedings of the Third Annual Institute on Psychology in Schools: Issues for trainers, administrators, and practitioners.* Washington, D.C.: American Psychological Association.

Tapasak, R. and H.R. Keller. (1995). A reaction to *where will* and suggestions for *how to*: The need to address systems level variables in school psychology role/function change efforts. *Journal of School Psychology* 33 (22): 201–208.

Thomson, S.D., ed. (1993). *Principals for our changing schools: Knowledge and skill base.* Lancaster, Pa.: Technomic Publishing Co.

Tyler, R.W. (1950). *Basic principles of curriculum and instruction.* Chicago: University of Chicago Press.

■ W, X, Y, Z ■

Walsh, W.B. and N.E. Betz. (1995). *Tests and assessment.* 3rd ed. Englewood Cliffs, N.J.: Prentice Hall.

Ward, M.A. and D. Worsham. (1998). *Student guidance and development.* Larchmont, New York: Eye On Education.

Ward, M.E. and B. MacPhail-Wilcox. (1999). *Delegation and empowerment: Leading with and through others.* Larchmont, New York: Eye On Education.

Worthen, B.R. and J.R. Sanders. (1987). *Educational evaluation: Alternative approaches and practical guidelines.* New York: Longman.

Worthen, B.R., W.R. Borg, and K.R. White. (1993). *Measurement and evaluation in the schools.* New York: Longman.

Ysseldyke, J., P. Dawson, C. Lehr, D. Reschly, M. Reynolds, and C. Telzrow. (1997). *School psychology: A blueprint for training and practice.* Bethesda, Md.: National Association of School Psychologists.

Zellner, L.J. and D.A. Erlandson. (1997). Leadership laboratories: Development for the 21st century. *NASSP Bulletin* 81 (585): 45–50.

Zepeda, S.J. (1999). *Staff development: Practices that promote leadership in learning communities.* Larchmont, New York: Eye on Education.